The Last Page of Michael's Diary

RiceDaddy7 Books

FIRST EDITION, December, 2016

Copyright © 2016 by Mike Leung

This novel is a work of fiction. All names, characters, places, and incidents either are products of the author's imagination or are used fictitiously. Any resemblance to actual events or locales or persons, living or dead, have been distorted in such a way that their identities and reputation are protected of the individuals they are based. The author holds all rights to this work. It is illegal to reproduce this novel without the signed and written consent from the author himself.

All Rights Reserved.

For information about interviews, book signing events, or special discount on bulk purchases, please contact **mikeleung5327@gmail.com**

Cover design and translation by: Louis Leung

Anchor ISBN: 978-0-9913809-6-1

Printed in the United States of America

In the summer of 2015, I had the opportunity to fly across the Pacific Ocean back to my hometown of Hong Kong. I also had the chance to visit Australia. In the span of two weeks, between the intensely hot weather and freezing cold temperature, I appreciated all the hospitality of friends and relatives. I'm especially thankful to Mr. Eric Lee for showing me the Tian Tan Buddha statue and later, Lantau Island where the area of Tai O and its Tai O Heritage Hotel were inspirations for this novel. The first draft was completed during my flight back to Los Angeles from Melbourne.

I also want to thank Ms. Cui-Xiu Yip and my son, Louis Leung for helping me edit and translate this book respectively. My son was very instrumental in helping it become available for print and digital. Without their help, the novel would not be completed in its final form.

Finally, I especially would like to thank my readers, whose support and encouragement have given me the strength to complete my story.

Thank you all,
- Mike Leung

Chapter 1

Nearly thirteen hours on the plane, I've set my luggage at the hotel and jimmied to the hospital where its uneasy stench awaits me. In one of its rooms lays the old woman, near-motionless and close to a hundred. Alongside her are her two daughters, bulky and far removed from their once slender and beautiful selves, but I, too, am no different. A glance in the sink's mirror reminds me that today I'm the half-balding, sixty-year-old shell, nearly unrecognizable from my handsome precedent.

Neither of her daughters would say hello, but I approach the old woman anyway, conjoining my warm hand with her cold, icy touch. I observe the old woman's frail state as she slightly pry her eyes open and gives an admirable effort to speak. She fails — merely an indiscernible whimper that becomes the produced effect. I try to make out the reply, but one of her daughter's thick hand intercepts the effort. Silently, I look up and remark to myself that she truly resembles her mother. This really is her daughter.

"Leave her alone," she commands, then adds, "She might get infected."

"Alright," I agree.

I sit myself down on one of the wooden chairs at the corner. We're now all sitting quietly, the dull atmosphere and expressionless faces making an already cold room colder. A nurse eventually comes and announces that she would re-dress the old woman. I excuse myself and exit to the entrance of the hospital. The humid noon air doesn't bother the passerbys. They are too engaged with life; too immersed in their own affairs.

Come sunset, I go to my hotel room where I try to catch some sleep, but either from jet leg or a heavy heart, I merely toss and turn until I end up returning outside. Even though the daytime has long passed, the city is baking like an oven. In Hong Kong, regardless of the hour, the streets are always crowded, unlike England where things properly end at nine o'clock and the only street occupants are mere homeless and drunkards.

Slowly, I follow the crowd's flow, drifting aimlessly until I stumbled upon an old noodle shop. Opening its heavy glass door, I immerse myself in its busy atmosphere. There are bustling customers and an equally scurrying staff and I choose a tiny table near a wall, returning a nod from a young woman sitting opposite of me. She was accompanied with whom I presumed to be her husband, a man whose expression suggests only imminent hunger. Simultaneously, a middle-aged waitress, whose grease-stained cloth is wiping away my grease-stained table barks, "What're you eating?"

And I reply with my best Cantonese, "Won...ton...noodles."

"What?!" She doesn't understand.

"Won...ton...noodles," I say clearer.

She comprehends after a pause and shouts at the cook, "An order for table number four! Wonton noodles!"

Her slang is difficult to comprehend and I only hope that she got the order correct. Two minutes later, a bowl of hot steam manifests on my table and the aroma of won ton makes me forget about Mrs. Wilson's table-side manners. Needless to say, it only takes me three minutes to devour the contents in their entirety.

Two days later, I revisit the hospital where I find Mrs. Wilson in her usual near-comatose state. After awhile, I stop visiting.

The following day, I go into a flower shop to buy a round of orchids. They were my mother's favorite flower. I remember from my childhood that my mother often stopped at a flower shop whenever we'd buy groceries. She often made conversation with the florist, but never bought anything from him. I later learned that it was because my father didn't give us much allowance; not surprising because he was gone a lot.

I remember how the florist would remark, "What beautiful hair you have, Michael. You know, tame hair makes for a tame child."

My mother would modestly scoff and counter, "Well, didn't you know the elders proclaim that children with curly hair and flat noses are burdensome?"

The florist smiled and lifted my chin, exclaiming, "His hair isn't that curly and his nose isn't that flat. You're a good boy, aren't you, Michael?"

When I heard his praise, I smiled like a fool.

"*Heh*. Like he'd dare disobey me?" quipped my mother.

And really, this was true. My mother was intimidating, more serious than most of my classmates' mothers. Her motto was: nothing is impossible; there's no excuse if we try.

This is my first return to Hong Kong since my move to Great Britain. It takes me four weeks to find the cemetery — its once distinguishable pine tree landmarks are now being surrounded by skyscrapers. Once there, I take out my loose leaf paper, the one with the lot coordinates that direct me to my mother's tombstone.

Once I find it, I admire the cypress tree I planted on the day of her burial. It was my uncle's idea to plant one next to the tombstone. I remember digging a hole for it with my bare hands while my uncle pleaded, shovel in hand, "Michael, do it right. Use this shovel. You'll get your hands dirty."

I ignored him, blocking all the sounds around me, tears streaming down my face. Finally, I lost all strength and succumbed to tears as I frantically shouted, "I'm sorry, Mother! Please forgive me!"

I didn't remember who pulled me out. Perhaps it was my uncle, perhaps it was someone else. All I knew was that it didn't matter.

Now that I'm at her grave, I silently observe the tombstone and wipe its contents with a handkerchief. Thanks to my sweat on the handkerchief, it makes the duty of cleaning the tombstone less of a chore. The tarnish helps uncover a black and white photo, encapsulating the image of my young mother, who died at thirty-five. The tombstone is engraved July 1, 1968. I stay until the early hints of sunset and then I give farewell with a deep bow. With a heavy heart, I leave the cemetery.

Back at the hotel, my wife texts me.

"Any progress with Mrs. Wilson?" she messages.

"Still near-comatose," I reply.

"Oh. Well, be sure to buy orchids for your mum's grave."

"Okay."

I didn't tell her I've already visited my mum's grave. I suddenly feel homesick and decide to check up on some flights back home. Luckily, it isn't peak season and there're plenty of availability. I can hop on a plane by tomorrow night.

During the next day, I go for a quick breakfast and make a return to the hotel. At the front desk, I approach a slightly chubby agent, her hair was pulled into a ponytail and the front of her bangs sliced into a perfect horizontal cut. She asks me, "Sir, can I help you?"

And I reply, "I'd like to checkout."

She makes a curious smirk when I say this, but I do not inquire.

"Of course. When're you leaving?" she asks.

"My flight leaves for the UK tonight. I'd like to checkout now."

The agent looks at the wall clock, then back to the desk monitor and exclaims, "I must inform you that noon checkout time has passed and you'll be charged an extra day if you leave right now."

"I see. I'll leave tomorrow then," I decide.

"Great," she smirks again. "I'll check you out tomorrow."

I grow irritated by her smirk and unleash my speculation.

"I've done something to your amusement, miss?"

With great embarrassment, the agent blushes, "Please don't take this the wrong way, sir, but we're having a large tourist group coming. Your room was in-between theirs and now, with it soon to be vacant, we've got conjoining rooms."

Her apologetic bow does nothing for me and I throw my ire.

"Miss, how long have you been working at this hotel?!"

"Three months," she fearfully replies.

"So you're still in trial period then?"

"Yes."

"Well, I think you lack professionalism," I seeth.

As my remarks were made, I notice several guests staring at me. Perhaps I should cover my anger by telling the agent I'm joking, but my phone rings and I scurry to answer it.

"Michael?" comes the voice of Lucy, Mrs. Wilson's eldest daughter.

"Yes?"

"My mother just passed away," she says. My heart sink. "Do you want to join us at the funeral?"

"Sure. I'll come."

"Thanks. I'll see you then."

After I hang up, I go back to the counter where I inform the poor agent I'll need to extend my stay. She blankly stares at me, not sure of how she feels.

Because the newspaper reports of a typhoon approaching Hong Kong, I had anticipated the gray skies to dampen Mrs. Wilson's upcoming funeral. Instead, it doesn't discourage turnout and there're plenty of speculators outside the church. I see Lucy and her sister, Susan, standing by the old woman's coffin. More guests pour into the funeral. Perhaps due to their affiliation for Chinese traditions, some columns are wrapped in white cloth and garnished with pale yellow flowers.

The two sisters are wearing all-black with a white collar. Their attire is complimented by a lone white flower, firmly sown to the side of their hair. In Hong Kong, this signifies a person who've recently lost someone. The entrance has a small table where a little girl pass pamphlets about Mrs. Wilson's life and all the guests are handed white roses because Mrs. Wilson was fond of roses.

When it's my turn, I bow three times to Mrs. Wilson, her corpse looking exceptionally serene. Lucy, too busy crying, does not acknowledge my presence but Susan gives me a hug. I feel a few tears from Susan and I pat her to comfort. Eventually, I find a seat in one of the corners, sitting next to a heavy-set man reading a pamphlet.

"Excuse me," he asks. "Aren't you one of Mrs. Wilson's students?"

I shake my head no.

"When I was in high school," he continues. "She was my teacher. All the students hated her."

Curious, I ask, "How come? She seemed rather nice."

"She pretended to be nice. Truth is, she was quite two-faced. I recall one time the entire class played a funny prank on her. She caught us and made us an offer that if we were to confess, she wouldn't report us. Well, we confessed and, well, she didn't hold her end of the bargain. We were all sent to the principal's office."

I add an inquiry, "Do you mind if I ask another question?" And without further waiting I ask, "If you didn't think highly of Mrs. Wilson, why did you come to her funeral?"

With that, the gentleman folds and pats the pamphlet on his hand. He points to a man in the distance, talking directly to Lucy.

"That's my boss," he says, handing me a business card. "He's the general manager of the real estate company listed on this card."

Hearing this, I reply, "I don't understand. What does this have to do with the funeral?"

"You might know that Mrs. Wilson owned a bit of property scattered among the areas of Central, Wan Chai and Causeway Bay." He sighs when he sees I don't get it. "Both my boss and I were students of Mrs. Wilson. We're here to get chummy with the property inheritors" — he nods at Lucy and Susan — "should they decide to sell them."

His words sadden me. So many people today are opportunistic rather than wholehearted. These cynical thoughts disappear as the priest and choir take the stage. I watch Lucy and Susan take their seats.

When the funeral finally ends, I attend the post-funeral dinner, a customary tradition called *jie hui jiu* — a feast to remove the bad spirits. I sit alone in one of the empty tables, but Susan comes and requests, "Why don't you sit with us, Michael?"

I shake my head, "No, I'm fine right here."

But regardless of that, Susan persists.

"Come on, Michael. I want you to meet my husband and Lucy's family."

I couldn't find any excuse after that to resist.

"Alright," I get up. "I see that you're in a better mood anyway."

She sighs as we walk towards her table.

"Today was actually liberating. The constant worries and visitations have taken their toll. All those nights staying half-awake in case of a dreaded hospital call..."

"Well," I comfort her. "All that's passed now."

Susan smiles and replies, "Yes. I have a Buddhist friend who constantly discusses life. Some things I agree; others, I find rather pessimistic. Like this issue with Mother, he offered me a few steps of advice."

This got me curious. "And what are these few steps of advice?"

"Acknowledge. Confront. Follow-thru. Letting go."

I thought for a moment. "Well, those don't sound too bad. They sound rather positive."

There's a glint to Susan's eyes as she looks at me and arrive at her table. A tall, athletic man immediately rises from his seat.

"You must me Michael."

"I am."

"Although these aren't the circumstances I'd have wanted to meet you, it's still my pleasure," he nods.

Susan plasters a smile. "It looks like you two have known each other for a lifetime."

"Well," jokes the big man. "Perhaps maybe I do know him and he just forgot who I am."

Getting his sarcasm, I smile and nod. Susan tsks and playfully smacks his bicep.

"Don't joke," she snaps. Then turns at me, "This is my husband, George."

We shake hands.

"Are you really Chinese?" I ask, fascinated by his unusual size.

George laughs.

"You're definitely not the first to wonder. There are many tall people from China, you know. Like me, I'm from Shandao. Professional basketball player Yao Ming is from Shanghai. Yi Jianlian is from Guangdong."

I'm embarrassed to be ignorant of professional basketball; my sport is really football and I didn't know who he was talking about. Fortunately, the big man reads my discomfort and changes topic, shifting to wine.

"I'm sorry," I apologize. "A majority of the people in England are accustomed to whiskey, actually."

The truth is, I actually abstain from drinking.

"No worries," George comforts. "I was quite the layman once as well, but over time, I've gotten to become quite an expert."

Susan scoffs, "Oh, don't listen to him, Michael." I watch her reach into his front pocket and pull out his business card. "He's got a business with an Australian winery — that's how he knows."

As I take the card, I realize how much Susan is using the opportunity to brag.

George inquires about my family.

"Six months ago, we sold our restaurant," he gloats. "We're retired now. How's your wife? Is she accompanying you?"

"No," I reply. "Our daughter just gave birth to our grandchild. My wife chose to stay in London."

"I envy you," congratulates George. "To be grandparents so young."

This naturally leads me to inquire about their child. Susan says he's running around somewhere. Lucy then shows up. She's accompanied by a thin-faced man sporting large glasses; I presume this to be her husband. The man, unlike George, was humble and soft-spoken.

"Lucy," I thank her. "I appreciate your writing to me on the candid condition of Mrs. Wilson. Had it not been for that, I wouldn't have been here."

Lucy's adult children join us not too long afterwards and the daughter introduces herself, "Hi, I'm Amy." She falls back, too shy to say anything else. I sense from her expression that the woman has much to ask me. I smile to ease her reluctance.

"Just call me old Uncle Michael," I offer. Then, a clumsy attempt at a Chinese pun, I joke, "In Chinese, my name is phonetically pronounced Mei Goh. Mei for 'not'. Goh for 'tall'. Not *goh* unlike your uncle George. And because I'm now old and expected to shrink, perhaps it's best you call me Mei Suk instead. Suk for 'uncle', but also suk for 'shrink'. Get it? Haha!"

They join me in pity laughter. Susan gets curious about how an Englishman like myself speaks Cantonese so fluently.

"Well, my wife's from Hong Kong originally," I reply. "And she makes me watch all these Hong Kong soaps. Then there's also my co-workers, most of them originally from here as well."

George carefully listens and mutters, "I see."

More people accompany us, but one in particular stands out. He has very long hair and thin glasses and I deduce right away that he's Susan's adult son. I remember seeing him in England so many years ago when he was a three-year-old boy attending Susan's father's funeral. I take the initiative to speak with the shy man.

"If I'm not mistaken," I say. "You must be Jack."

A blushed nod was his only response.

"Yes," I confirm to myself. "You are Jack. All those years ago in Britain. Well, time certainly flies and I feel old."

Susan agrees. "You're telling me. Sometimes I wish he'll be my baby boy forever."

Knowing he's now the subject of attention, Jack feels embarrassment and pushes away his mother's hand.

"Mother," he pleads. "Please stop."

It's clear to me now that even at forty-years-old, his mother represses Jack's growth. Eventually, both Susan and Lucy leave us to greet other guests. George joins them and I am alone with Jack. He attempts to say something to me, but I have to lean to hear him.

"Mister...Uncle...Michael. I-I want to go to the UK, b-but my mother forbids me. Can you speak with her and p-perhaps change her mind?"

He notices my hesitance and sits closer. I smell the presence of strong cologne, which makes me a bit uncomfortable.

"U-Uncle Michael," he attempts again. "I-I won't bother you in England, I swear. I-I've got a good friend living in M-Manchester."

When I distract myself with a pouring of tea, Jack does the pouring for me. I respond, "How did you meet this friend?"

Jack blushes and answers, "A-at a bar, sir."

I smile and guess, "At a gay bar?"

"W-well..." Jack corrects me in near whisper, "Actually, i-in Hong Kong we call them Comrade Bars."

This lifestyle is common in England, but perhaps in Hong Kong it hasn't really been socially accepted yet. It may have led to Jack's apprehension. I let the thought linger in my head as the real estate agent from the funeral slides next to me.

"Wow, Michael," he admires. "I've no idea you were so close to the Wilson family! Please let me know if you could put in a good word for me!"

I ignore him for the rest of the *jie hui ji*. After the feast, I return to the hotel.

Chapter 2

Back at the hotel, I bump into the same receptionist, this time sporting her hair minus the ponytail and accompanied by a silver clip. She matches my glance, then turns away intimidated, as do the other front desk agents. Perhaps I've developed a reputation. Someone who I presume to be the lobby manager approaches me.

"Hello," he plasters a smile. "I'm Mr. Liu, the lobby manager of this hotel."

I politely nod to him.

He continues, "I must apologize on behalf of my staff the other day. It was all a big misunderstanding. Perhaps I can upgrade you into a penthouse suite facing the sea?"

"I appreciate your sincerity, Mr. Liu," I nod. "but honestly, I was just giving your agent a hard time the other day. Please don't read too much into that."

Mr. Liu continues his insistence up to the elevators and I shake my head and return to the counter. The staff appears intimidated and I assure them, "Please, relax. All of you. I'm not here to start trouble."

They offer a bewildered silence. I pat the manager on the back and calmly explain, "I once owned a restaurant in England. I understand firsthand that the customer must be made to feel like royalty. Your performance, while lacking in professionalism, was made under the thoughtfulness of guests. Your hearts are in the right place."

After hearing this, the staff cheers up and applauds my assessment. The hefty teller clasp her hands and makes a bow of appreciation.

"To make things easier for your situation," I add. "I'll be heading back to England tomorrow."

After finishing this remark, my mood immediately lightens; I've made the right decision. I book a flight to London upon returning to my hotel room.

―――――――――――

After breakfast the next day, I encounter the same receptionist at the counter. Her mood was much brighter and, revealing two brilliant dimples, greets me with a big smile.

"What's your name?" I casually ask.

"Oh! My name's Ally," she answers without eye contact.

"Oh! Ally. I'll just jot down your name and write a good word for you when I get back to London."

Politely, she thanks me. Back at the room, I pack whatever's left and the manager knocks to inform me that a shuttle bus has been called to take me to the airport. While waiting for the shuttle bus, I sit at the hotel's cafe, reading a book I purchased on a stop from India. I flip no more than two pages when a pair suddenly approach me. Instantly, I recognize them.

"George...Susan," I greet. "I hadn't expected you."

The look of Susan's expression tells me this wasn't a friendly gathering. A medium-sized package drops on the table and it sends my coffee splattering. I immediately produce a napkin to wipe off the spill. Still, my mind remains baffled — what could be the reasoning behind Susan's outrage? Her husband softly eliminates the mystery.

"Are you taking my son to England?" George asks.

So that's what this is about.

I immediately reply, "Jack merely came up to me that day and asked about it."

"No," snaps Susan. "That's not what my son told us. He said you initiated the idea."

"What the hell? Susan, if I was really planning that, wouldn't your son be here, waiting for the shuttle bus with me?"

They look at my solo luggage, realizing that I'm telling the truth. Embarrassed, Susan realizes her mistake and apologizes, "Forgive me, Michael. You know how much I love Jack. I overreacted." She points to the package on the table, "Anyway, this is from my late mother. We found it while cleaning her belongings. There were specific instructions to give it to you."

I look at the package, then return a puzzling glance. George only offers back a clueless expression and Susan shrugs at my reaction.

"Don't ask me what's inside. I don't know either," she says. "I'm just following her instructions."

"So...you mean..."

"Yes," she finishes my thought. "It means take it back to England and open it there."

"Wait," George asks with sudden bewilderment. "You're really going today?"

I respond, "Yes — is something wrong?"

He scoffs in disbelief, "Well, didn't you see the news? There's a strike at the airport."

My God! If that's really true then I've no idea what to do! I immediately call my wife and verify the news. After the call, George knows from my expression that I acknowledge it to be true. I excuse myself to the lobby to think. Asking the manager for a few nights was now out of the question, since the large tour group that Ally described has already arrived. I see them, sitting in the lounge, pacing back and forth — the hotel is bound to be soldout in the next few days.

Sigh.

Along with the mysterious package and the strike situation, I really don't know what to do! I think back to George and Susan. I beg them with pleading eyes to help me find a place. George contemplates, stroking his chin, then he makes a phone call. He signals for Susan and I to be silent as he mumbles to the other end. The noise from the lobby forces the big man to migrate to my cafe table and we follow him as he continues his call. He subconsciously takes my glass of water and drinks it at one point, but I don't stop him. Finally, the call ends.

"I've got good news and bad news," informs George. "Which one would you like to hear first?"

Irritated by his tease, I'm tempted to pour my coffee over him. Instead, I play along, "The good news first."

"Okay," he slowly replies, still dragging the answer. "The good news is that after a lot of work, I found a beautiful four-star place, a natural environment where you can catch a beautiful sunset."

"Wow," I'm awestruck. "With such an appetizing description, what could be the bad news?"

The truth is, I've grown tired of Hong Kong and its drab buildings. A beautiful, natural environment sounds absolutely delightful.

"The bad news isn't actually quite so bad," George shrugs. "It's just that it's a bit far from key points of the city."

I immediately rebuke, "That's no problem. In England, every place is a 30-45 minute drive — an hour if you take the train."

George smiles.

"Good. Good. You didn't know how difficult it was securing that place...it has limited rooms and, well, luckily someone cancelled at the last minute."

I see from the cafe window that the shuttle bus has arrived. I apologize to the driver for the address change. George helps carry my luggage into the shuttle and then both he and Susan join me in the ride.

George chuckles and says, "Don't worry, Michael. I've already told the driver the address."

With my helpless situation, my faith is placed on the couple. The shuttle moves westward as I observe the thermometer next to the windshield: 34° C. I look outside the window and see the smothering sun baking the city. It's a contrast to the ride's atmosphere, the relaxing blast of the air conditioner and smooth commute. I rest easily, feeling like a child rocked by his mother's arms.

Not knowing how long I've slept, I wake shortly afterwards and observe the steel bridge our bus passes. I admire a speeding ferry underneath us, its trial illustrated from a pair of white streaks. I also notice the traffic signs that indicate we're close to the airport and I ask George, "Why're we still heading to Chek Lap Kok?"

Half-asleep, George suggests, "It's alright, Michael. We're going the right direction." I watch him return to his slumber and I feel embarrassed to have bothered him in the first place. I, too, go back to sleep.

Around twenty minutes passed when the shuttle abruptly stops at an unfamiliar bus station. We're jolt awake and begin removing our luggage from the back of the shuttle. I look in all directions and...everything seems familiar all of a sudden. As I try and recall the destination, George pats a large hand on my shoulder and Susan grins, "Do you remember this place, Michael?"

Not able to exactly recall, I respond with a head shake.

"It's alright," George waves. "Come with me. Let me show you a place."

Dragging my luggage with me, I follow George past the bus station and into an area of running speedboats and an aroma of salty fish. The area's windy. At the turn of the corner I see a river with lots of dingy stilt homes; it's all a display of minimal living under the poorest conditions.

Now I know where we are.

"This is Tai-O," I realize.

George nods.

"You've arranged for me to stay here?"

George nods again.

"My God, are you kidding me?!" I protest.

From behind me, I hear Susan snickering.

"George," I sternly insist, "if I have to pay more, I'll do it! I'd rather live in a more accommodating area! There's no way I'll stay here and stand this horrible fish smell day in and day out!"

With a burst of laughter, George whisks my luggage and runs off with Susan to a nearby market area. Among narrow streets full of patrons and makeshift restaurants, I fight past packed crowds as most onlookers scratch their heads and wonder why three sixty-something-year olds are running like children. Not that it matters to me. I keep sight of George and Susan and fortunately, my football playing days with my two sons has kept me in shape. The couple's old bodies soon betray them and Susan succumbs to a nearby chair. George does similar. Half-a-minute's all it takes for me to catch up.

The three of us immediately burst into laughter and it's the happiest I've been in the trip. I can barely breathe as Susan apologizes to the shop's proprietor and buys three mountain begonia drinks for a hundred HK dollars. Through thirst or heat, I quickly devour the delicious sweet and sour nectar. Susan orders three more.

"Don't be so modest, okay Michael? I insist you take these to the hotel."

I thank her. "This is like the blackcurrant drink from England."

The shop proprietor eavesdrops and nosily adds, "Yep! Here and Ngong Ping are the only parts of Hong Kong you can get that mountain begonia drink! Why, I picked the begonia myself from nearby Phoenix Mountain!"

"Oh. Is...that so?" I carelessly dismiss the prying shopkeeper.

We ignore her for the rest of the conversation.

"Sigh," Susan chimes. "It's been awhile since we've had such a wonderful time, Michael. I wish Lucy was here to re-live our childhood. Don't you remember, Michael? How, after school, we'd play football in that small hilly field? You were so tiny back then, but you were always the goalkeeper."

She lays back on her chair and gets lost in a distant memory. I plaster a polite smile, knowing we're remembering a revisionist recollection. The truth is, I've never forgotten what really happened;

it's been in my heart for a lifetime. Susan and Lucy probably hated me as children, made me play goalkeeper just to intentionally kick the ball at me, hurt me, kick the thing out of bounds so I could scrub my knees to pick it. Oh, how they'd laughed manically. Mother would find scratches and bruises when I returned home. It hurt to see Mother's discomfort.

"Hey! Why don't we head toward the hotel?" George breaks the silence.

He stands up and I follow him with my own luggage back in hand. Tai O evokes memories. I pass by a small house that serves as a makeshift temple —the same one my maternal grandmother used to take me. I remember its small bamboo stages and the Cantonese opera singers entertaining the passing crowds. My grandmother used to enjoy them here.

We walk further past squatting fishermen playing mah-jong in a tiny courtyard. Two dogs lazily sleep beside their table, half-listening to the cling and clacks of the game's tiles. Then, something hits me — the scent of baking shrimp paste. Somewhere in the distance I know it's being made. I recognize that smell because I'd spent a summer making it, back in my junior high days. I took a job to save for an electric guitar, the months of sweating and suffering just to hear that crisp electric sound. I remember crying like a happy fool when I obtained it.

A partially lame man, approximately in his nineties, approaches me and interrupts my daydream. The old man produces a rolled paper with silk ribbon tying it and before I grab it, Susan pulls me aside, "Don't do it. It's a trap. He'll then frame you."

Not quite understanding her meaning, we clarify in English.

"What do you mean he'll *frame* me?" I ask.

"Well," she whispers in English. "It's more like he'll force you to buy what he's holding. You break it, you buy it."

To our surprise, the lame man replies back in English, "No, I'm not a scammer. I just want to give this to you. It's a drawing. Please don't judge things so quickly."

Susan's stunned by how this Chinese man, with his sullied appearance and attire full of holes, can speak English with such Oxford purity. That unexpected surprise, however, is not enough to persuade us to take his gift. We leave the old man by hurried pace, knowing he couldn't catch up. I pity him for trying. The area's now more naturally scenic and less occupied. We're closer to the water and, as we turn the corner, another unexpected surprise await — though, I really should've expected this one. I've lived in Tai O as a youth, but never laid eyes on its reconstruction. No longer are shrimp paste farms contaminating the air here. We're isolated now, quiet as heaven. We enter an area full of familiar ancient trees and the boundless sea that accompanying our way toward a steep hill. From a distance I see that old pier, its newly refurbished state and its well-crafted posts lined up like chained pawn pieces and the pier itself, a loyal lover, firmly standing to await its betroth's return. With the low tide, I'm able to see tiny crabs — sand crabs, the locals call 'em —scurrying among the earth's crevices. The path merges with the ancient tree roots. I believe most of them are centuries old.

We stop in a heavily shaded area, enjoying the cool sea breeze. Susan stands motionless, but George disregards etiquette and frees his belly.

"Ah! It feels so damn good," the half-shirtless George exclaims.

Susan disapproves and buttons back his shirt, "Please show our guest some courtesy."

"What's the big deal?" George retorts. "Michael's family."

Susan finishes and looks at me, pointing upwards toward the hill. I recognize it.

"Do you recognize this place?" she asks.

I silently nod and glimpse at where Susan was pointing. I see it — nearly hidden among the giant trees is that familiar white fort; an old police station that I knew in my youth. We're near a steep driveway that serves as both a pedestrian and vehicle entrance toward it. As we walk upwards on this driveway, we pass a peculiar sign that reads, "TAI O HERITAGE HOTEL". I can hardly believe they've converted that thing into a four-star hotel.

When we arrive at the top, the bellhops hastily take our luggage and lead us to a cramped lobby. I recognize it; this is the old police station reception area. It's more of a small room now, with a tiny sofa capable of seating three adults. Crammed in the paltry area is the old report table that now serves as a check-in desk and two tiny jail cells adjacent to it, now only for show. There's a makeshift stand that carries brochures and travel guides. I admire some retro photos neatly arranged on one of the former station's freshly painted walls. A few of the brochures detail the fort's history and preservation. The receptionist hands me some guest forms as several staff stand ready to enter my data into a computer.

"How long will you stay here, sir?" we're asked.

Too distracted by the furbishing, George replies for me.

"Let's set it for a week, but make it flexible to go beyond that. Is that okay with you, Michael?" asks George.

"Sure," I mutter.

A nostalgic thought slips into my head and I creep a naughty smile, suddenly crouching under the former police report table and pop up at the receptionist. I burst into a deviating laughter as the receptionist and staff collect themselves.

"S-Sir," the receptionist inquires. "Are you insane?"

I smile and bask in their fear, looking at their concerned faces which only Susan finds amusement.

"Oh, such a child you'll always be, Michael," she jabs. "Will you climb on the desk too?"

With only the two of us in amusement, I suddenly look frightened.

"What is it, Michael?" she asks. "What do you see?"

I burst into laughter again and say, "I see an Indian police officer!"

Susan roared in hilarity.

Chapter 3

After saying farewell to George, I give Susan a hug and tell her, "Thanks for arranging this stay. There're certainly many memories from childhood here."

Susan coolly replies, "Think nothing of it. They merely had an available room; it was an easy favor." She casually observes the hotel and mutters, "Too many memories, for sure." She leaves with her husband and promises to see me once more before my departure.

I know she doesn't really mean it.

The staff helps carry my luggage to my room. While usually my first action is to set my towels and toiletries, I, instead, leave my things this time and observe the exterior of the hotel. I walk along its terrace, admiring the majestic nature of its colonial-age arches and columns. It's amazing how this fort was the anti-thesis of a cold police station and now, equally unexpected, a luxury resort.

As I made my way towards the Tai O Heritage Hotel's entrance, I stop and observe some elementary students visiting on a field trip. They're scattered impatiently, some even escaping into the lobby to elude the mid-summer heat. I watch as their poor teacher shout and bark orders until a whistle finally assembles them together. One-by-one the children line up and follow them to the lobby.

A juvenile thought creeps upon my mind as I shut the lobby door and pose as an arriving guest. The children resume their rowdiness, scattering across the small room, mostly playing in the former cells. They climb and cling to the swinging jail doors, pretending to be prisoners and policemen. I feel bad for the poor teacher as she valiantly tries to bring order from the chaos. At least there aren't other guests to witness this spectacle — although the employees are irritated from their expressions. We watch as the hapless teacher bring order to one cell only to find the other one reinvigorated.

Suddenly, a scream pierces the lobby and I see the receptionist trying to stop a child from climbing the former complaint desk. *Hah!* At least it's not just me who finds it tempting for horseplay. Perhaps it attracts children through curiosity. Back in the day, the desk was so fun to scare people. I remember once in my youth I tried to scare whoever was on deck and caught myself staring face-to-face with an Indian sergeant. I've never seen an Indian before and his unusual appearance sent me crying. All the officers laughed at me.

"Children," I suddenly have a thought, waving at them. "Would you like to hear a story?"

I watch as they continue to carouse and clown, but one girl approaches and solemnly asks, "I heard this place is haunted. Is it a ghost story?"

As she says this, other students are interested and repeat in unison.

"Oh, no, no," I assure them. "There're no ghosts here. The only stories I tell are relevant to facts."

From a distance, I see their teacher smile and appreciatively nod.

"If you're interested," I wave for them to accompany. "Follow me."

I take them outside, confident of my familiarity with the layout. Although much has changed since its renovation, I know the fort's details are probably still intact. Just on the side of its exterior, I found it — the bullet hole. A boy walks up and rubs the tiny crater. The children are engaged as I theatrically explain an old shoot out; coppers and robbers, fighting to the brink in a true adventure. I re-enact this epic battle, playing both roles to the applauding amusement of the children. I lead them around the corner next to the second-floor restaurant and its adjacent cylindrical observation deck.

A boy asks, "Sir, if pirates had appeared back then, how would the police have dealt with them?"

It gladdens me to know that today's generation are so inquisitive. I praise the child and reply, "Good question. When you all came up from the driveway, did you notice anything peculiar?"

Silence. Then, the same girl who asked about the ghost stories replies, "A giant cannon!"

I nod and compliment, "Close — it was a small cannon. But you see, children? This girl is very observative. You should follow her example and notice things around you."

As we part ways, the teacher approaches and exclaims, "You were truly a big help today. I thank you. May I ask if you're a teacher? The way you communicate, your extensive knowledge — "

I smile and stop her, "I'm merely a retired person, ma'am. I've lived at Tai O. My experiences can far surpass whatever information's in that folder you're holding."

"Yes, well, I'm very grateful," she agrees.

"May I ask your name, Miss — ?"

"Au. My surname is Au. And you're...?"

"Just call me Michael. It's a pleasure to meet you, Miss Au."

She extends her hand and I set my drink down to shake it.

We bid each other farewell.

Back in my new hotel room, I begin organizing my clothes and other personal belongings. I whistle merrily knowing that the simple things are what gives life joy. Clothes are placed in hangers to preserve their pristine ironing and when I'm done, I give my undivided focus on Mrs. Wilson's cardboard box. I whip out a small letter opener and remove the airtight taping, finding no gold or silver, nor title deeds or stock shares. Instead, there are only a handful of diaries, mine — and my father's. I give a double take, surprised that Mrs. Wilson kept his diaries. They're methodically organized, year to year, making it easy to find the one I'm most interested.

The year was 1968; my happiest year, as was my saddest.

I remove its protective wrapping and both a black-and-white photo and contest application falls. I was the one who placed them there; I know what's in them. The black-and-white picture features five young aspiring musicians — the youngest being shy me, holding my then-newly purchased electric guitar and the two long-haired blokes being the then-boyfriends of Lucy and Susan. Lucy and Susan made up the rest of our young crew and behind us is an older gentleman in large-rimmed glasses. I take the contents to bed and lay there reminiscing.

It's a Saturday, Mother is playing mah-jong at Uncle's house and I sneak out with electric guitar in hand. I dash all the way to the pier, taking a boat ride to Central where the rest of the band awaited. During the ride, I deliberately undo the top two buttons of my yellow leather jacket, popping my collar to exhibit a more untamed appearance. I thought about sporting sunglasses as well, but amidst the day's cloudy conditions, reconsider it due to people mistaking me blind. As the boat docks, I walk across Queen's Road, basking in the attention that not even one pair of eyes from the young

women there fail to notice me. In truth, I'm freezing my fanny off; it is one of Hong Kong's coldest winters.

At one o'clock, our band have used its studio time and transfer the booth to the next band. The five of us are in the lounge room, drinking water and packing up things and I'm carefully putting away my beloved electric guitar when suddenly Susan yelps. We follow her line of vision and grow excited to see Uncle Lou, the director of Hong Kong's most famous radio station, walk into the lounge. Everyone knows that if Uncle Lou signs a band, it will surely go Top 10 within a week.

He politely greets us.

"Hello, Uncle Lou," we excitedly reply.

"I'm just here for some coffee," he assures us. "Hope you don't mind."

We watch as he tossed an old pot and began a new brew. Our eyes never leave him as he presses the MAKE button. With empty cup in hand, he notices our quiet admiration and exclaims, "I saw your session. You kids have talent. May I offer a suggestion though?"

Of course, no one will dare tell the most powerful music personality no.

He continues, "Indeed, you all sing well, especially this young lady who sounds like Diana Ross of the Supremes. It's no wonder during practice you covered 'Stop in the Name of Love', but see, that song requires a female chorus and, well, between all your male members, the sound comes across as a bit weak."

I quietly glance at Lucy and Susan, the latter's wide eyes starts drifting to the ceiling; I know she doesn't find the critique complimentary. Susan loves the Supremes. She sings their songs in her friends' parties and often forces Lucy to dance and sing with her.

The station director backs off. "It appears my words have offended. Should I seal my lips?"

"Oh no, of course not," comes Lucy's boyfriend, Dennis. From the couch, he hastily shoots up and goes to comfort her. Her head is now sunk and displeased with pride. "We're all grateful for your suggestion, sir," assures Dennis.

"Good. Well, I think you play drums very well," Uncle Lou looks at Dennis. "You've got a great sense of rhythm. And you, young man —" he points at me.

"His name's Michael, sir," informs Dennis.

"— Michael, your guitar playing's a bit soft. Put some oomph in that strumming."

A staff member pops in and interrupts the commentary.

"Uncle Lou," he blurts. "James is on the phone. He's looking for you."

With a playful wink, the director leaves the lounge. Lucy didn't wait a moment too soon to declare, "Even if he really is a big shot, who the hell is he to tell us what to do?!"

"He's a good friend of your father's," Dennis informs.

"What?!" Lucy asks in disbelief. "Are you sure?"

"Yeah, don't you remember your father in every China Fleet Club's Christmas performance? Listen — I heard rumors that Uncle Lou got drunk once and pissed off some triad members. Thanks to your father's intervention it was the only reason he left that incident untouched. As a gesture of gratitude, Uncle Lou helps announce ticket sales each year to the China Fleet Club. I hear they sell out as fast as half a day."

Lucy snorts, unimpressed.

"So?" she remarks. "What's that got to do with us? We don't need him."

Dennis sighs.

"Don't you get it?" he pushes. "Look, we can do petty school performances all day long, but this guy's the big time. You know how much we could make performing at the China Fleet Club? Foreigners and high class locals — they all attend that thing!"

Unconvinced, Lucy injects, "Regardless, I still think he's rubbish."

Just as we're ready to leave, Uncle Lou reappears and hands us a stack of applications.

"There's a singing competition this year at the Hong Kong Festival," he explains.

Confused, Susan asks, "Hong Kong Festival? I've never heard of it."

"It's a series of government sponsored activities next winter," says Uncle Lou. "There's going to be music, parades and other activities I can't currently recall."

Lucy, still unconvinced replies, "What does this have to do with us? The thought of competition never entered our plans."

"It's the perfect opportunity, my dear girl. If you land in the top three spots of the music competition, the record companies will sign you — this is your chance to shine."

This interests Dennis who intervens, "Is there any song you'd recommend for us to cover, Uncle Lou?"

With some contemplation, Uncle Lou have his answer. "I've got a song that'd be perfect for you guys, though the drummer must be well in rhythm." Our eyes suspense-fully cling to him as we wait for Uncle Lou to reveal this selection. He excuses himself and comes back with a vinyl record. As it spins around the record player, grainy sounds and catchy drum beats fill the room.

"Wait/ oh yes/ wait a minute Mr. Postman...," comes the lyrics.

Dennis begins singing, though struggles to recall the song's name.

Knowing it is one last year's Top 10 songs I blurt out the band, "The Beatles."

"I know!" Lucy completes my answer. "It's 'Please Mr. Postman'."

Uncle Lou gives her a thumbs up as he crosses his arms and rocks in rhythm. We sing and clap along with the song and as it ends, the station director puts an arm around both Lucy's shoulder and mine and asks, "So what do you guys think, eh?"

Dennis loves it, but Lucy frowns in dissatisfaction, letting her opinion known that the song is geared towards male voices. Uncle Lou immediately interjects and explains, "This song was originally sung by a female group — The Marvelettes — in 1961. The Beatles merely made it mainstream. Combining both genders, with a female lead and a male group backup...it would be an amazing fit."

We consider his proposal.

"By the way, what's your band's name?" Uncle Lou asks.

We shrug.

"Huh," he laughs surprised, "a band without a name? That's interesting."

"Well..." I explain. "We've came up with several, but we couldn't agree on one."

"Like — ?"

I boldly give out some of our more audacious ones, "Like, uh, The Hong Kong Britains...or...or...The Cockroaches. You know, like there's the Beatles, so we could be the Cockroaches."

Everyone laughs. Tears of laughter comes streaming out of the studio director as he removes his glasses and wipes his eyes. He resumes, "Alright, I've got a good name and I hope you'll all like it." Walking between Susan and Lucy, he announces, "Your name is Lucy and yours is Susan...so...LUSAN — AND THE THUNDER!" He waves majestically at the air and awaits our approval. "What do you think, hmm?"

At this, Lucy gives an approving grin.

With both arms still around the girls' shoulders, Uncle Lou pulls their heads closer to his.

"So you kids'll return here next week?" he appeals. Knowing our answer, he adds, "Next Saturday, then. I'll introduce you to some professionals. They'll really polish up your singing skills!"

We spend the following week wondering who are these 'professionals'.

Come Saturday, we arrive earlier than usual and find the recording studio packed. When it's our turn at the practice booth, we encountered two men and a woman who are still inside. Their dark complexion and slender builds have us guessing they are Filipino. As soon as they saw us, they greet us in Cantonese, "Hey there. I'm Tony. Which one of you is Dennis?"

Like a child answering a teacher, Dennis raise his hand in response and Tony walks over.

"Tony," he reiterates and shakes Dennis' hand. "These are my friends and band mates. We hail from the Philippines.

Let me introduce you — our lead guitarist, Roy. This beauty right here's Irene, our singer."

After further introductions, he urges us to perform, but Lucy declares herself unready and mysteriously runs to the lounge. Tony and his friends, perhaps too used to this in their show business career, impatiently pick up their instruments and start singing. I watch Tony start banging the drums and Irene putting the mic to her lips.

THUM-THUM-THA-THUMMM.

"Wait/ oh yes/ wait a minute Mr. Postman...," sings Irene.

"...Mr. Postman/wait and see/is there a letter in your bag for me?" hums the two Filipino boys.

Their style is smooth and strong. Dennis begins singing, but quickly stops to mimic Tony's drumming. The door is left ajar and I notice a prying audience in awe at the Filipinos' spellbinding performance. Lucy storms back and reclaims our privacy.

"Holy — wow!" Dennis cheers as the song ends. "You guys are great!"

I agree. I, too, am in serious awe. Roy's fingers have flown up and down his electric guitar and his natural grace makes me feel amateur in comparison. As I clandestinely pack my own guitar, a large hand interrupts and leads it back out of its case.

"What do you think you're doing?" Uncle Lou scolds. "You came here to practice, not attend a performance."

He hands me back my guitar and I sheepishly take it. Uncle Lou continues, "Whatever you may think of yourselves, know that these are professionals and you'd do well to follow their dedication. Drop your pride and take this session seriously and perhaps you'd come out on top at the festival." He looks at Tony, "Tony, it's your job to take care of these...adolescents." The Filipino band leader returns an A-ok gesture.

"Sure, Uncle Lou," nods Tony. "You got it."

As Uncle Lou leaves, the three of them become our personal tutors. I am very attentive to Roy's guidance and whether or not it was through inspiration or his actual teaching ability, Roy has me playing with confidence. Even stubborn Lucy learns new tricks from Irene as she taps into her diaphragm and emphasizes more soul in her voice. Both Lucy and Susan are taught to dance in-sync to their singing.

"Alright, everyone," Tony declares. "Let's put together what you're taught."

Tony claps for us to begin. It was amazing how under the same song and the same group members, we are able to sing at a whole new level under their guidance. Uncle Lou shows visible excitement behind the booth window. He's clapping and cheering us on as we finish with immense confidence.

At an Easter concert, we're outperforming even the main act. After the show, Lucy and Susan merrily hops onto their mother's car and I wait impatiently for the last bus to the ferry. There are only fifteen minutes left for the final boat and I grow worried of missing it. Amidst my anxiety, a familiar white Mini-Cooper pulls alongside me and a voice orders, "Come on in."

Mrs. Wilson rolls down the window and I see Lucy and Susan in the back seat. I accept and plop into the left passenger seat. This is my fourth time meeting Mrs. Wilson — Mother has told me my first encounter was when I was a baby, but my first recollection was when I was five and my father took me to her house to play with Lucy and Susan. The second time was one of Lucy's birthday parties; that particular day, my mother came and argued with Mrs. Wilson...though I can't really recall why. I remember they were in her dining room, Mother screaming with finger-wagging succession and Mrs. Wilson, calm with arms crossed, smugly sitting on her couch. Initially, Mother was screaming in broken English but as she struggled with it, she switched back to Chinese cursing knowing that Mrs. Wilson understood it quite well. It was like an unstoppable force battling an immovable object. Eventually, Mother dragged me away and ordered I'd never associate with that woman again. We'd left so early, I didn't even try the cake. My third encounter, we had just formed our band and practiced at Lucy and Susan's house. Their mother had returned from her trip to England earlier than expected. This was my first face-to-face with Mrs. Wilson. We made pleasantries, I remember, and perhaps she didn't recognize me and thought I was just another one of her daughters' friends.

That night in the Mini-Cooper, Mrs. Wilson doesn't say much to me. She isn't even responding to whatever chatter comes from Lucy and Susan. When we arrive at the ferry station, we learn that the last boat have already departed and an old sailor, pipe in mouth, is found closing the gate.

"Michael," Mrs. Wilson suggests. "Why don't you stay over at our house for the night?"

I sit dumbfounded, not knowing how to explain Mother's disapproval. Mrs. Wilson, reads my expression and assures, "Don't worry, I'll inform your father and he can tell your mother where you're staying, okay?"

I draw a sigh of relief, knowing my father has a way of calming.

The following afternoon, Mother doesn't scold nor speak to me— I know she isn't happy with what happened. During dinner, I deliberately tell some frivolous gossip, but Mother has none of it. She sternly plantsd her chopsticks and handily remarks, "Michael, I know about your passion for music and

I don't mind it or your acquaintance with that *damn foreigner*'s girls, but understand something...your entrance exams are coming soon and you should be taking studying a lot more seriously. That's why —"

She goes on as my gaze drifts. Slowly, I stare back and met her stern, icy expression. I'm so intimidated, I scoot my chair over.

"Remember what I'm telling you today," Mother articulates. "Because I won't repeat it."

I shrink and nod.

"If you don't make the top of your class," she threatens. "I'll take away that guitar."

Even today, I can feel the chills. I still think about that moment a lot.

Chapter 4

Ring! Ring!

The caller ID displays my wife's name.

"You're not asleep?" I answer.

"Maple just took back the baby. Since she dropped her here so late, I really thought she'd leave the baby with me."

I laugh. "Well, it would've been great if our granddaughter stayed. You'd be less lonely tonight, with me not being there and all."

Amusement coms from the other side.

"Well," my wife chuckles. "If I could choose between the baby and you coming here every night, you wouldn't stand a chance."

Ha! Thinking about our grandchild really makes me homesick.

"Have you heard from the news when the strike'll end?" I grumble.

After a brief silence, "Well, on the telly the union said it'll be sometime this week."

Sigh.

I take a stroll down the terrace with phone forged into my ear. The view of the sunset's spectacular — a red sky dyeing the flock of clouds crimson. I describe the imagery but my wife jokingly accuses me of exaggeration. We soon bid farewell and I enjoy the sunset alone. I observe the pier's habitants — some fishermen and a young couple holding hands. The man is lugging his backpack while the woman sports an open cerulean-dotted umbrella. Their unusual attire is peculiarly outdated, particular the woman, whose red long-sleeve shirt and bouffant skirt reminds me of Audrey Hepburn-era fashion. I watch them make their way towards the Tai O Heritage Hotel and then stop at its entrance. The woman poses — umbrella across her back, hand grasping at the umbrella's edge — as the man takes out an easel and draws her. I observe. Throughout it, I only see the woman's back. A sprinkle of people pass by them without mind. It eventually drizzles and I return to my room tired.

Came near nine o'clock, I awaken from my brief slumber and fancied a nibble. Unfortunately, the restaurant staff is vacuuming and putting away dishes. A waitress, complete with plastered smile, informs, "Sir, we're closed."

"I thought this place closes at ten," I assert.

She apologies. "We close at nine on weekdays."

I glance at a large clock and see its hands pointing five 'til nine.

"I don't mean to be bothersome, miss, but it's not quite nine and I do apologize, but I'm rather hungry. Can I please trouble the chef into making me something?"

The waitress took some pleading to follow-through. I finally watch her go into the kitchen and return nonchalant.

"I'm quite sorry," she informs. "Most of the chefs have already left, but we've some cold dishes, if that's alright."

"Salads, sandwiches and the like?" I made sure.

She nods.

"Well, then," I smile. "Trouble whatever chef to make me a Club Sandwich — extra mayonnaise, a dash of mustard."

The waitress gives off a peeved grimace. I sigh and lighten up, "How about just any sandwich then? I don't want to be a nuisance."

Ever since the check-in prank, I've made myself ease up on the staff. Running a restaurant has also given me some empathy with the service industry — I know, for instance, that chefs get irritated easily. My compromise gives the waitress relief and I sit near the window and gaze. For a moonless night, the stars sure give the sea a nice splattering of silver. A couple minutes pass and the waitress returns with a plate of sandwiches — the anxious staff did a good job. The French fries are crisp and the pickles, well-sliced.

"Any accommodating wine?" the waitress suggests.

"No," I reply, "but some hot coffee, if you don't mind."

I haven't drank since my father killed himself by collapsing drunk off a bar stairway. Those familiar with me know this to be my true reason, but for others, I give off health reasons. The coffee comes after I finish and, because I'm well-rested and imbued with caffeine, signal for the tired waitress to dismiss her.

"I won't hinder you further," I promise. "Usually after a meal, I sit awhile and grow lost in my thoughts. Perhaps you should be on your way."

I generously tip a 100 HK dollars and watch her thank me. She offers more coffee.

"No, it's fine," I initially say, then thinking better of it, "Perhaps, later."

"But, sir," she pleads. "We need to clear out guests before closing."

I nod and negotiate, "Very well. I'll sit outside."

"I'll leave you with a coffee pot and access to the machine."

"Fine," I nod. "I'll be sure to shut it off when I'm done."

"No need," she grins. "Our night staff will handle it."

Excellent.

I sit and watch the lights go and their staff leave one-by-one. The manager departs last and checks the door three times to confirm it's locked. As I'm alone, the darkness consumes me in all directions save for a lone lamp beside my wooden table. Fortunately, hotel music cuts through the silence and the sprinkles of street lights and lucid stars share the burden of luminosity. I sip my cooling coffee and recall what a frequent customer at my former restaurant told me. The customer, an elderly widow, was alone after his daughter married and moved to Northern Ireland.

"Michael," he advised. "Be prepared to embrace the loneliness as you get closer to your twilight years."

Now, I truly grasp his words.

With the cicadas chirping and the random dogs barking, the night sky becomes a blanket and it sends its demons of destitute and dismay. I close my eyes and succumb to the helplessness, re-opening them moments later to find a synchronized companionship between the stars, lights, croaking frogs and serenading cicadas.

Realizing this, the loneliness fades.

My favorite song is heard playing as I take another sip of coffee. "Nothing Can Stop Us Now" was an Australian song by Rick Price and written by the late-composer Paul Damien Gleeson — a talented man whose life was cut short by cancer. I continue enjoying the tune and sip my coffee until the song ends. I get up, take a stroll downhill and walk near the pier where I stumble upon the earlier young couple. The artist is now sitting at the pier's stone steps with the Audrey Hepburn-era woman leaning on him. They say nothing, enjoying the crashing of waves. A gust of sea wind suddenly blows and the man re-fixes her hair.

I leave them to their privacy.

Returning through the Tai O Heritage Hotel lobby, I glance at its wall clock and notice it's 1:15 am. In my room, rather than sleep, I decide to skim through my diaries, giving up at just two pages. I read Father's diaries instead, starting from the earliest — the year he was transferred to Hong Kong. I begin reading page-by-page until the first hint of sunlight seep through the window and I temporarily fall asleep, awakening to the persistence of my growling stomach.

Not taking the chance of another near-closing, I hustle towards the hotel restaurant, feeling relief to find it half full of patrons. The same waitress from last night seats me at a round table and exclaims, "I knew you'd sleep late last night."

"Actually, I didn't sleep until morning," I reply.

"Wow," she remarks, surprised. "Why didn't you sleep longer?"

I point at my stomach and she laughs understandingly.

"Gotcha," she nods. "I presume you won't be choosing Club Sandwiches?"

"'Course not," I scoff. "Recommend me something — what's good?"

The waitress smiles. "Everything here's good."

I can tell she wasn't lying from her hefty looks.

"How about you tell me what guests usually order?" I advise.

She flips my menu to the Lunch Specials and points at a combination.

"That set, sir."

"Alright, let's do that set then."

"Soup or salad?"

"Soup. Any soup will work as long as it's hot."

She jots down my choice. "And what of the main course? Fish and Chips or fried rice?"

Knowing that the Fish and Chips here is probably not as good as the ones from home, I easily pick the fried rice. The soup turns out to be mixed vegetables and when I finish it, the following plate proves quite pleasing to the eye — fried rice, scallops, shrimp. The problem, however, is that it also comes with a strong shrimp paste odor.

The waitress notices my disapproval and chimes, "Sir, you initially might not like the smell but you'll quickly get used to it. Trust me."

I keep my cynicism.

"Just take a bite," she insists.

I sigh and conservatively succumb to her persistence. Clutching the small napkin with my right hand and picking up the fork with my left, I take a small sample of the dish and prepare for an embarrassing regurgitation. The paste, though, swims in my taste buds as the familiar expectations of shrimp, rice and scallop suddenly combine for an exotic flavor. I slowly put my fork down.

"P-Perhaps Fish and Chips would be more to your liking," the waitress begins as she slowly starts removing the dish.

I clutch her arm to stop her.

"Actually," I smile. "I'll just need a bigger fork."

She laughs and our banter draws the attention of other guests. After my meal, I take some Lipton tea without the milk and sugar. When the bill arrives, I see that the waitress is disappointed with my twenty percent tip. To be honest, the gratuity's already included and she should be happy that she's getting anything additional. Perhaps I've spoiled her with my previous 100 HK.

Back in my room, I continue my reading of Father's diary, devouring its contents 'til the last page.

No.

I stop and toss it back into the cardboard box. I stall time by going to the restaurant for a cup of coffee, hoping the caffeine will sooth me, but it pumps my adrenaline instead. I put down my cup and found courage to finish Father's diary. Back in the room, I whisk it back, slowly absorbing the final page.

...

...no.

— *Why?*

Oh, dear God, why'd I read it?

All these years...why had I done what I'd done?

Chapter 5

That night, I can't sleep. Fragmented memories keep me awake until the dawn of morning. But just around noon, my slumber falls short by outside cheering and joking. Even though I try hard to sleep again with covered blankets and pillows, I'm unsuccessful. I call the front desk to complain, but no one answers. I make myself proper to complain in person, but by then it's already quiet. Seeing how I'm already decent, I decide to head to the hotel's restaurant to find the source of the chattering. The obnoxious group's so loud, their voices consume half the restaurant. I grow annoyed at this and attempt to leave, only to find them heading towards the exit with me. I give it a second thought and let them pass so I can stay at the now-quieter restaurant.

"What an annoyance," mutters the familiar waitress.

She's now to the side of me as I sit down.

"Do they come often?" I inquire.

"Not that particular group, but the tour leader's a mainstay. He'd bring a new wave and every time they're here, they're irritating. His groups just sit and never order."

"Because of the prices?"

"Well, this is what they say..." she pulls over a chair and imitates the tour guests. "I CAN'T READ THESE WORDS!" she sits and exaggeratingly barks in Mandarin Chinese. She slams the menu and I pick it up to notice Chinese words next to the English. Knowing what I'm thinking, she continues her imitation. "THAT'S NOT THE CHINESE WORDS I'M USED TO! I ONLY READ SIMPLIFIED CHINESE!"

I laugh because I understand her annoyance.

After lunch, I stay at the restaurant rather than head back to my room. I witness the afternoon sun being covered by a looming black cloud and soon, the low pressure makes the air stuffy, causing me some mild suffocation. Ten minutes later, raindrops the size of raisins mercilessly pound the restaurant's windows. The scenario fogs up and is barely visible. I notice from a distance the same familiar couple — the artist and woman with the dotted cerulean umbrella — casually walking with disregard to the current weather. The rest of the people, though, are scrambling for shelter.

The wistful backdrop suddenly gives me an idea. *I ought to combine the diaries.*

I return to my room, plop open my laptop and sit towards the back window. For the next fifteen minutes, I contemplate how I'd weave Father's stories and mine together. The rain stops and I observe its leftovers shedding from the roof.

I blink and the back window show an older version of the fort's entrance.

Below, on the ground floor, is an Englishman, hurriedly approaching the original fort doorway. He puts down his umbrella and brushes the condensation off his shoulders. He takes out a letter and happily reads it.

At least — this is how I imagine it occurred.

The Englishman is James Wilson and the letter's from his wife, Margaret.

"Dearest James,

We've been apart for two weeks now. London's weather remains predictably gloomy. The morning fog especially makes everyone unhappy. Whenever I think of you, I feel lonely. This semester's seen an unusual amount of foreign students — most of whom are from countries that speak little to no English. That's why they've implemented an ESL program and they've chosen me to teach it. To be honest, I wasn't quite sure if I could handle it, and after a week, I now understand what you've went through in your early days in Hong Kong. Communication is a challenge. Luckily, these students have been wonderful and learn much faster than I expected. One day after class, I made conversation with one of these foreign students: a girl from the New Territories of Hong Kong. When I brought up where you worked, she said she'd never been to your area, but she knew that Tai O was a fisherman's village. She's been living in the New Territories all of her life in Hong Kong. "

I imagine Mr. Wilson nodding and thinking, yes, Tai O's a small fishing village with a tiny population. Due to its location southwest of Hong Kong, the island is valued for its shipping channels. That's why the government set up a Marine-based police station to guard its vessels.

Mr. Wilson eagerly takes the initiative to reply:

"Beloved Margaret,

Did you know, your letter made me happier than I expected? Prior, I desired an immediate return to England, but this job currently offers more incentives and opportunities from Commissioner McGrady. Furthermore, the savings I receive from all the perks and benefits allow me to save and, therefore, end up with more than the previous job at home.

Besides, the people here are courteous, even if communication is a bit challenging. Luckily, there's an Indian sergeant who can speak Cantonese on my behalf. And my own Cantonese is improving too — at least to the point where the other officers are afraid to outright utter 'that damn foreigner' without me knowing. I know this distance is hard on you, Margaret, but I prefer to temporarily work here. I can save for a nice house, just like the one your father has in the suburbs.

Let me tell you another positive, I've recently stopped drinking. It's rather difficult to find a tavern here in this small island. Instead, I've spent my time practicing my guitar. There's a monthly club for foreigners in the Wan Chai district for local Englishmen and boorish Americans. One of our band members is a colored American who plays a brilliant jazzy tune with his trumpet. Everything I've done in Hong Kong, I've jotted in a diary. I'm hoping to read it to you when we next meet.

Revered Margaret, I will love you forever and always.

- James

March 21, 1950"

And here is where Mr. Wilson seals his letter, writing the address tidily in a sealed envelope. He falls asleep.

The following day, I imagine him personally ensuring the letter is sent by walking three miles to the post office. The postal workers inquire why he doesn't use the porter. Mr. Wilson merely smiles because previously he had used one, but later discovered the porter hadn't even sent the letter. "So what, *damn foreigner?*" was all the porter muttered and that's why Mr. Wilson insists on sending the letters himself.

Two weeks later, Mr. Wilson receives another letter from his wife — he's ecstatic.

"Dearest James,

Today, I've got good news, Mum took me to see Dr. Campbell and he informs me that I'm pregnant! The baby's expected at Christmas — hopefully you'll be here during that time so it can feel like a present. Although Mum and Dad have kept me company, I really want you to be here during our child's birth."

Mr. Wilson feels both happy and sad after reading this and immediately begins two letters. The one to his wife comprises of joy and pleasure; the other is to Commissioner McGrady which requests a transfer back to England. He tosses and turns that night, conflicted with the excitement of having a new baby but also apprehensive to wear the ol' black uniform again — the one where he patrolled London's merciless cold winter. He then remembers his promise for always being there for Margaret.

At the China Fleet Club, the club he mentioned in his letter, he looks all over for Commissioner McGrady, but after half-a-day trying he's unsuccessful.

"Have you seen, Commissioner McGrady?" he asks around.

The bartender takes one look at his uniform and ignores him, but an eavesdropping customer strolls over, drink in hand, and informs, "Commissioner McGrady's been busy. All these incidents with Mainland Chinese smugglers have taken his time and given him a headache."

"I know how it is," nods Mr. Wilson. "There've been a lot of activity with the Mainland Chinese sneaking into our borders. I know he's busy, but I've got an urgent request. Do you know where I can find him?"

"Well," contemplates the stranger. "I heard he's facing the media today, probably talking about securing the borders. If anything, you should try the headquarters. That's where he'll likely be."

As Mr. Wilson leaves the bar, he sees the Commissioner exiting a lift. The commissioner makes a beeline towards the bar, ignoring Mr. Wilson as he plops on a couch, lost in stress. With application in hand, Mr. Wilson hesitates to bother his boss, but the waitress near the commissioner notices the sergeant's apprehension and makes the commissioner aware of his presence. The commissioner looks at him and beckons him over. Mr. Wilson's desire to see his wife again gives him the courage to hand over the transfer request, but no longer than he reads two pages, the commissioner angrily tosses it back and barks, "You bloody no-good wanker! Why don't you take this bloody letter and go back to your bloody fisherman's post where you belong!"

Embarrassed, the sergeant leaves the club in disgrace.

On a ferry to Tai O, the waves' tumultuous nature reflects the state of Mr. Wilson's heart. He grows agitated as the ride gets closer to the fisherman island and he rips the transfer request to shreds. The pieces scatter across the winds and land in various parts of the sea. He sighs and looks at the sky, hoping that the commissioner will be in a better mood in their next encounter. But alas, I imagine him, doomed and sighing as he probably sees the last remnants are now behind the ferry, symbolizing his procrastinated hope. As soon as he takes a seat, however, Mr. Wilson notices a distant tugboat that perturbs his instinct. Alarmed with a bad feeling, he quickly makes his way to the ferry's captain and urges him through fragment Chinese to stop. Gesturing, he radios a transmission to the island's police station, requesting a convoy dispatch for the suspicious tugboat.

Less than a minute, however, the tugboat tilts and its passengers begin screaming. The good sergeant urges the ferry's captain to pull closer for a rescue. As the ferry gets near, the small boat is already half sunk and dozens of its passengers struggle afloat. I can see Mr. Wilson now, cool-headed, taking the initiative by tossing life savers to the few who managed to swim by. For the rest, he and a few volunteers take off their shirts and dive head-first into the water, life savers in hand. The coast guard arrives and each and every passenger is saved.

A tragedy prevented, Mr. Wilson swims back to a standing ovation.

Back to his living quarters, the good sergeant writes about the incident to his wife. He stops short, though, on mentioning the conversation with Commissioner McGrady because he doesn't want to disappoint her.

The next day, he sends the letter then walks to the police station. As soon as he enters, the desk copper, Wah Chai, informs him that the commissioner called twice looking for him. The sergeant better return the calls, Wah Chai suggests.

"Okay," Mr. Wilson complies, dialing the Commissioner's phone immediately.

"I knew you'd call back, Wilson," grumbles Commissioner McGrady. "I need you to come to the main headquarters at noon."

"Yes, sir."

Right before Mr. Wilson hangs up, the Commissioner adds, "And wear a nice uniform when you come."

"Yes, sir."

From his office, Mr. Wilson examines his wardrobe and takes out a clean uniform; one that wasn't worn and torn from the daily grind of working at Tai O. He adjusts his tie and makes his way to the headquarters in the main island. When he arrives, Commissioner McGrady is there. The Commissioner immediately pops from his desk and greets, "Wilson! Glad you've arrived." Then, inspecting a gold watch. "Right on time. Let's go meet the press."

"Yes, sir," Mr. Wilson complies, still unsure of what's happening.

The Commissioner leads him to an underground area where both local and foreign reporters await. Some are from prestigious presses like Time magazine and Reuters. I imagine Mr. Wilson, trepid and silent, standing next to Commissioner McGrady as the Commissioner details the previous day's rescue. He reveals that the rescued are actually refugees from Mainland China. The speech paints Mr. Wilson as a hero and after the press conference, the sergeant is taken aside and offered to drink with Commissioner McGrady at the China Fleet Club. A feeling of elation seeps in Mr. Wilson as it renews ample time to repeat his transfer request.

At the China Fleet Club that evening, Commissioner McGrady orders his usual whiskey on the rocks, but Mr. Wilson hesitates to order.

"Is it alright if I don't drink?" appeals the sergeant.

The Commissioner appears offended. "And why's that?"

"Because," Mr. Wilson replies sheepishly. "I'm not able to hold my liquor, sir."

The commissioner laughs hard, holding his belly. He appears jubilant, certainly the most audible at the China Fleet Club.

"Well..." the commissioner rolls his eyes then turns to the bartender. "Hey Susie! — Give this bloke some whiskey. But no rocks. Change it to Whiskey on Water."

Mr. Wilson observes his boss being the happiest he's seen.

"You know, Wilson," smiles the Commissioner. "That heroic deed you did yesterday, with the boat and all, you really did me a big favor. The press had been hounding me on our handling of those Communist refugees. They said we weren't compassionate. Well, that little act you've done...that made us look real good."

He takes a sip of his whiskey and gestures for Mr. Wilson to do the same.

"Ah," the Commissioner basks. "So — that little letter you gave me yesterday. What's the reason behind the request?"

Mr. Wilson smiles and finishes the rest of his Whiskey on Water. He fully discloses his reasons but the Commissioner stops him short.

"No," Commissioner McGrady cuts him. "Absolutely not. Forget those promises you made your wife. Bottom line, Wilson, I can't let you leave."

I see the sergeant's expression livid, outraged. He forgets his rank and blurts, "Then I quit — sir."

The Commissioner chuckles and calms him down.

"I won't let you leave, Wilson, but I can certainly arrange for the missus to be with you at Tai O."

The sergeant isn't sure how to take the offer.

"Even if I agreed to that, how could my wife live with all the men down at the dorms?"

"Why, she'd be living in the family dorms, of course."

Mr. Wilson chuckles, "The family dorms?! But sir, we both know those are reserved for the higher ups. A lowly sergeant like myself — "

The commissioner leans and gives an assuring pat.

"Oh, it won't be a problem anymore...*Chief Inspector* Wilson."

The sudden news exhilarates the former sergeant and I see him abandoning his emotions. He grabs the commissioner and delivers a shocking kiss, full beard and all.

"I-I-I didn't expect to be promoted so soon!" cries Mr. Wilson. "I can't wait to tell my wife!"

The commissioner watches him float with euphoria and celebrate around the bar. He immediately summons the bartender.

"Susie, how much whiskey did you give that bloke?"

"Just the usual, sir," she replies. "Half and half."

"Well next time, make it a quarter," the commissioner wipes his face. "My God, can that man really not handle his alcohol!"

    The bartender laughs.

Chapter 6

Nearly three months later, Margaret Wilson arrives to Hong Kong. From Father's journals, I'm told she and her husband are carried throughout the Tao O piers in litters: wheel-less vehicles carried by human transport. Their litters are adjacent to each other as Mrs. Wilson hold hands with the recently promoted chief inspector, delighted in the ambiance of royalty.

One night, in the balcony of their new dorm, the Wilsons sit amorously as Mr. Wilson holds his wife's hand and places his other one on her belly.

"Hello, young fellow," he whispers to the stomach. "I'm anticipating your arrival." Then, looks up to his wife and declares, "Margaret, I promise to be a good father to him. I'll show him how to play football and ride horses so that when we get back to England, he can join our niece in riding her pony. That pony's quite well-behaved, you know, beautiful and white — tame and appropriate for children."

His enamoredness is met with contrast to his wife's impassiveness.

"What's wrong, Margaret? Was it something I said?"

"Yes," she nods. "It was."

"Please, what is it? What did I say to offend you?"

Mrs. Wilson takes a long pause and stares at the streets and its many pedestrians. After a moment she replies, "You really want our child to be a son, don't you?"

Mr. Wilson chuckles, "Well, either a son or daughter's fine."

"Oh, really?" she looks at him in grave seriousness. "You've been using the word '*him*' throughout our time together."

I imagine another chuckle coming from Mr. Wilson as he attempts to defuse the situation, "Honey...come on, I sometimes forget how, as a teacher, you cling onto every detail. *Him* is generic. How about from now on I refer to our baby as 'our child'?"

She laughs, perhaps to be amiable, but I guess earlier that afternoon she'd seen a doctor and was probably told the baby will be a girl. But Margaret knows her petulance doesn't help, so she offers an olive branch, "I'm sorry — I was being a bit cross, James. I know how much it means to you that I carry a son."

Before he injects, she stops him and continues, "You're from nobility — you want to extend your heritage. I understand that."

The chief inspector wraps his arms around his wife and assures, "Honey, don't question. Whatever our child ends up, I'll love you both with all my heart." Changing the subject, "Darling, don't you notice the streets are busier than usual?"

She leans towards the balcony and observes her husband's assertion; there are, indeed, plenty of adults and children. The children are all carrying different types of lanterns. Mr. Wilson points to the full moon and explains, "Tonight's their Mid-Autumn Festival."

"Really?" gasps Margaret. "This is a Hong Kong celebration?"

"It's celebrated by the Chinese everywhere."

He points to one of the lower balconies where a family is enjoying moon cakes. Suddenly, with a light bulb popping on top of his head, Mr. Wilson grasps his wife's hands and leads her to the street. Margaret hasn't a clue of his intentions, but smiles at the joy surrounding them. Along the road are plenty of children holding lanterns in various shapes and sizes. Some are starfruits and lotuses; most of the boys prefer aircraft-shaped lanterns while the girls seem to prefer decorated traditional-shaped ones. The smaller children hold white rabbit lanterns as they bounce around their older siblings. Margaret falls in awe with the culture exposure. Her husband later takes her to his former living quarters, the one he shared with eight to nine Chinese officers as sergeant. The old dorms are empty save for three remaining officers who probably have no family to share the holiday with; they're going about their cooking as if it were any other night.

I imagine one of them, Wah Chai, is cooking among

the heat sans shirt and he suddenly feels embarrassment seeing the new boss and missus. He quickly rushes to cover himself, but Mrs. Wilson tries to tell him it's okay and she and her husband are the ones at fault for showing up uninvited. Mr. Wilson translates her message with basic Cantonese and the officers laugh and invite them for dinner. Mrs. Wilson grows curious towards what they're eating.

"James, darling," she points. "What's that dish with the brown sauce?"

"Steamed Pork with Salty Shrimp Paste," replies her husband. "Seems like you're interested."

His wife laughs.

"I just want to try it," she shrugs.

"Impossible," Mr. Wilson says mystified. "How could you possibly want that? It smells like rotten meat inside a toilet."

But Margaret ignores him and, with an amateur's grasp of chopsticks, takes a sample to try it. The combination of taste and smell pleasures her, so Wah Chai, seeing this, scoops some rice into a bowl and gestures her on how to properly eat it.

"He's telling you it goes better with rice," explains Mr. Wilson.

Not used to properly grasping the bowl and chopsticks, they give Margaret a spoon to eat the pork and rice. As Mr. Wilson watches, he's reminded that women develop different tastes with pregnancy. Wah Chai, seeing the new chief inspector holding nothing, quickly fetches some beer.

"Chief Inspector," Wah Chai announces, bottles in hand. "Seeing how the night is celebratory, let's all have a drink."

Mr. Wilson initially refuses, but then gets lured by the low extent of alcohol and how it'd go well with the fried cuttlefish.

"Bottoms up!" they all shout. "Happy Mid-Autumn Festival!"

Since the Wilsons have only one bottle each, they remain sober as the rest continue drinking. Not long afterwards, the lone phone rings and a tipsy Wah Chai stumbles to answer it. He mutters and slowly hangs up.

Mr. Wilson walks up to the officer as Wan Chai returns to his meal.

"What happened?" the Englishman asks in his best Cantonese.

"Aw, one of the officers left his post to handle a bunch of rowdy teenagers by the shoreline," Wah Chai explains. "So now we've got a report from his empty post and they want us to handle it. It's probably only bickering; you know how it is, boss. I wouldn't make it life or death."

The new chief inspector goes over to the phone and calls the Tai O station for clarity.

"This is Chief Inspector Wilson, I want to know what's going on," he asks. "...yes...yes...I see. Alright, I'll be at that abandoned post in five minutes."

He takes his wife and her handbag, ushering her to leave. Confused, she doesn't know what's going on until they arrive at their room and Mr. Wilson explains.

"I see," the missus realizes. "Well, you better go to the incident, then."

The abandoned post consists of an area of makeshift homes comprised of poorly aligned sheet metal. One of them is full of shouts and screams. Mr. Wilson ducks his six-foot-two frame into its half-opened door, witnessing a crowd surrounding two women: a scrawny twenty-year-old lass cursing and grasping the shirt of her stout middle-aged adversary.

As soon as they're aware of the presence of the high-ranking British officer, the women immediately stop fighting. Mr. Wilson asks the situation in his best Cantonese, but I see them trampling over their own answers. He tells them, in English this time, to speak slower. The scrawny arguer, making the best of her limited English begins to explain, but as the tall chief inspector ducks to hear the tiny woman, the stout arguer stops her opponent in fear that she might be poorly represented.

"Humph!" barks the stout one. "Don't think just because you can speak to this *damn foreigner* that you can get away with what you've done! There're witnesses here knowing you started it!"

At the sound of 'damn foreigner', Mr. Wilson lights up and warns the stout woman in broken Cantonese, "Anyone...who...calls me...DAMN FOREIGNER...will...go to...jail!"

This threat freezes her.

Soon afterwards, a squad of policeman approach the home and relieve Mr. Wilson.

At the foot of the hill is a chapel, whose brick and wood was brought and converted by Father Gordon and members of his church. As it's the only church in Tai O, both locals and foreigners believers conjoin for worship every Sunday. It's also the only place Mrs. Wilson made friends. Father Gordon is one of them, an Irishman who've settled in Hong Kong for the past thirty years and, consequently, spoke fluent Cantonese without a hint of accent. The other two friends are Jennifer and Johnny, an elderly couple from Texas who currently lives in the more mountainous areas of Tai O.

Whenever Mr. Wilson doesn't accompany Margaret, the elderly couple takes the initiative to bring her home, flourishing a friendship with their half-hour walks. Interestingly enough, Father Gordon doesn't take a liking to the Americans, often citing them as rude and mock the two with an exaggerated Texas accent.

One Sunday, I imagine Mr. Wilson getting the day off and attending mass. From the diary, it's said that the Americans stop the Wilsons after service to make small talk. Margaret grows curious after a few snacks and asks the elderly couple why they'd chosen Tai O.

"Ah," laughs Jennifer. "Don't you know? It's absolutely tranquil here — and if we want to go to areas like Central, it's just a small hop on the ferry."

Margaret tilts her head, "But there're plenty of peaceful places in Europe. Italy and France, for instance. Charming fishing villages. And even in the southwest side of England, there's a quiet fishing place called Cornwall. James and I spent a vacation there before we were married."

The old lady tsks and replies, "I dunno. Maybe growing up in Texas has made us uncomfortable with Europe's cold weather. Why, one winter I recall freezing in Switzerland during my younger brother wedding — don't laugh, it's his fourth one."

Something tingles Margaret's female intuition, "So I'm guessing you're in your 70's and your little brother is...in his...60's?"

Jennifer giggles, "Well, Robert's twelve years younger and I'm seventy-four so — sixty-two."

"And how old was the bride? Young gal, I presume."

"Oh — she was a year older."

They both laugh.

Johnny grows impatient with the gossip and interjects, "Why don't you tell her what happened at the wedding?"

Jennifer pats Mrs. Wilson's hand to apologize.

"Oh, forgive me, Margaret. I've jumped ahead of myself. The wedding was at a castle on top of a snowy mountain. — Oooh, it was so scenic. Everything looked beautiful, including the bride who looked so young that day. The make-up artist really did a great job — Ah. I'm drifting away from topic again." Jennifer's expression suddenly turns sullen. "Okay, so, during the ceremony, Johnny's head droops to my shoulder and I'd thought it was maybe because the sermon had bored him. So I nudged his head and — guess what? — my hand was wet and I noticed he was unconscious and drooling. Now, I used to be a nurse and I recognize the signs of a heart attack. Fortunately, one of the guests was a doctor and got Johnny first aid and an ambulance."

"Yep. I wouldn't be here if it weren't for that doctor," scoffs Johnny.

"Yeah," Jennifer nods. "We later found out cold weather triggers his heart and upon the advice of a doctor, avoided cold weather since."

Margaret blinks, "But...I mean, surely Texas isn't cold, is it? I hear it's in the south part of the United States. And it's quite large."

"W-Well, we're actually from Galveston," stammers Jennifer. "A port town by the Gulf of Mexico. It started as a modest slave trading post, but a century later, during the oil boom, it grew quite rambunctious and...well...all those ships and construction... it just became too loud." She looks at her husband and expresses, "We like Tai O a lot. We're gonna live here 'til we die."

Johnny agrees.

"And your adult children?" Mrs. Wilson pries. "Don't they contact you?"

"Well, they've got families of their own," smiles Jennifer. "We let them be."

Eventually, the Wilsons bid goodbye and head home where Margaret muses about their conversation.

"She's right, you know — regardless of male or female, children will eventually leave on their own."

Mr. Wilson smirks, knowing her implication. They pass through various areas until they stammer upon the same cluster of sheet metal homes that Mr. Wilson investigated during the Mid-Autumn Festival. He points this out to his wife when footsteps interrupt and a voice beckons, "Sir — SIR!"

They turn around to see a young Chinese couple, both dark-skinned and very thin. The man approaches and extends a hand.

"Chief Inspector! " he greets in English. "I'm William Chen. People just call me Chen. I teach English at Tai O."

"Is something the matter?" asks Mr. Wilson.

The English teacher points to his girlfriend and says, "She's my student and also my lover."

The girl shyly nods, "We've met before, Chief Inspector."

Mr. Wilson curiously tries to recall her, though aside from various degrees of height and weight, all Hong Kong women seem to have the same flat facial features.

"Perhaps we could invite you both for refreshments?" offers William.

He points towards a small, rundown makeshift cafe a few feet from them. Normally, Mr. Wilson reserves a distance toward the locals, but seeing how the two seem kind and that his wife is probably tired from walking, Mr. Wilson accepts the offer. As they approach the makeshift cafe, he sees three tables; two of them are dirty and the other is occupied by children doing homework. The Wilsons choose the less dirtier one, the table without the garbage. The owner, upon seeing the presence of a foreigner, immediately stops her mah-jong game and rushes toward her new customers with barely her slippers properly worn.

"Yes! — Sir!" the owner bows in basic English.

William explains they're merely there for refreshments and, hearing this, the owner immediately grabs a towel and wipes clean their table. As she returns with soft drinks, William asks, "How much?"

"Oh! It's in the house!" she insists. "Anything for the chief inspector!"

William pays regardless.

Margaret whispers to her husband, "How much do we owe William, James?"

"The officers don't usually ask to be paid back in these instances."

Unsatisfied, Margaret takes out her handbag and begins sifting through it.

"Please!" she insists, waving a handful of HK dollars. "Accept our payment. I'm sure one day on the job you'll be in my husband's debt."

Her persistence catches William off-guard and he feels embarrassment. He takes the money from Mrs. Wilson while his girlfriend, in broken English, explains, "This...my request...I...bring...William...speak you..for me."

The Wilsons silently sip their fizzy drinks, anticipating the couple's solicitation.

"Her name's Ho Yin Di," explains William. "The night that the chief inspector came to our home, Ho Yin Di was fighting her step-mother."

Mr. Wilson suddenly recalls this and asks, "Yes, what was that ruckus about?"

"Oh, just a mere, common argument," William waves off.

"Well, if it was so *common*, why bother reporting it?"

"How about if I start from the beginning...?" William points at his girlfriend. "We all call her Di. She grew up in the fisherman life. Her mother passed away when she was three and left her with a one-year-old brother. Soon afterwards, her father remarried to that same hefty woman you stopped that night — together, they had a son...a son who took the looks of his mother. On the night of the Mid-Autumn Festival, there was a high tide which meant plenty of fish swam near the coast. Because her father has asthma and it acts up during the weather change, her step-mother insisted that her little brother take his place, but my girlfriend wanted her step-brother to go instead."

The girl immediately interrupts and injects, "Yeah...I want brother to study. Why...my brother...always...fish? Her son...always study?... I want...them...switch."

"Di..." Mrs. Wilson mused. "I like that name. It sounds like Judy. Mind if I call you Judy?"

The girl hesitates and agrees for politeness.

"So — Judy," continues Mrs. Wilson. "On the night of high tide, why didn't you just go in your brother's place?"

"Oh," William rushes in. "That's because she has a sensitivity in her ear. Like vertigo. I forget the scientific name..."

"Ménière's," Margaret nods. "It's named after a French doctor. Ear imbalance."

"Yes, madam. That's why Di is unable to go to sea."

Margaret nods and sinks the explanation — then gets to the nitty gritty.

"So what can we do for you today?" she asks.

Judy jumps up and hollers, "I...want...job. Home. *Dead fat po*...bad."

"*Dead fat po*...?"

Mr. Wilson immediately slaps on the table and howls at this wife's confusion.

"*Dead fat po* , haha, is their slang for Damn Fat Woman. Don't you know that?!"

"Mmm. I see," his wife says, unfazed. "I get it now. Dear, please refrain from rudely embarrassing me in front of company again."

Mr. Wilson stops and composes himself.

"So," Margaret turns back to Judy. "You want my husband to find a job for you?"

"Just...police station...I can clean..." Judy makes clear. "Have...dorm there. Can live..."

Mr. Wilson listens patiently, "Well, we do have a janitorial opening, but it wouldn't suit you. There's a lot of heavy lifting involved."

The girl's raises her expression and pleads, "Sir...please...I no go to school...but...I work hard...I clean all area of police station...at home...I pick up heavy...for father..."

Margaret injects, "James is right. It really wouldn't be suitable for you. Besides the physical work, you'd also be living with a bunch of men. Isn't there something else in the city that'd fit you?"

"I...don't...want...to be far...from brother..."

Margaret empathizes, "I understand. How about next time at church, I'll ask for available jobs?"

The words comfort Judy and the girl jumps to elation. She bombards the Wilsons with nonsensical gratitude and William speaks on her behalf.

"Yes...she can take care of children, " William explains. "She raised two brothers. In fact, if you'd like, even now she can be of assistance to your pregnant wife."

"No, it's fine," waves off Margaret. "Thanks for the offer — I'll be okay. But I'll ask for job openings."

Chapter 7

After the Mid-Autumn Festival, Hong Kong has grown a little colder, though the ocean breeze keeps Tai-O warm. The sunsets paint the horizons red and the Wilsons delight in them, often sharing the balcony to watch the sun disappear. As its absence is felt, the temperature drops, but the nights are still warmer than their accustomed Novembers. Mr. Wilson looks eastward at the crescent moon, a symbol that reminds him of cradling. He momentarily leaves the balcony and returns with his guitar.

"Sweetheart," he suggests. "I really want to sing for you tonight — the song from when I proposed."

He begins to strums and sing, but Margaret suddenly stops him.

"B-but," he protests. "This is your favorite song. Why'd you stop me?"

She playfully kisses him and replies, "Darling, I loved it then, but now that we're married, its significance has served its purpose." She laughs at his daze. "Why don't we sing something else instead? Let's sing something together."

Mr. Wilson plants a kiss.

"Alright, dear. What do you want? British or American? Folk or popular...just don't ask for anything difficult."

Margaret smiles, "Well, I've got a song in mind. A simple one...not too difficult."

He scrunches his face. "Give me a hint. What's the song?"

She points at the sky.

"Ah," Mr. Wilson guesses. "'Somewhere Over the Rainbow' by Judy Garland."

"What? — No. There might've been a rainbow this afternoon, but there isn't one now, silly."

"Mmmm. I don't know then...I've drawn a blank. Can you hum it?"

She ignores the request and begins pointing at various areas of the sky. Mr. Wilson observes, then gets her meaning. He strums from his guitar, then picks up the easy tune.

"Twinkle, twinkle little star," they both sang. "How I wonder what you are?/ Up above the world so high/like a diamond in the sky./ When the blazing star is gone/when he nothing shines upon/then you show your little light/twinkle twinkle all the night."

Margaret kisses him.

"James, I'll always remember this moment as the first song we've sung for our child. I'm certain *she* was singing along with us."

He touches her belly.

"I feel the same way, my dear."

They reflect on the crescent moon, imaging their baby in its embrace, accompanied by the flashing stars.

One early evening, Mr. Wilson returns home and quickly changes. He takes a fizzy drink from the refrigerator and stands at the balcony with a solemn expression. Margaret sees him and knows something must've occurred at work. She finishes making dinner and gently approaches.

"Dinner's ready," she announces. "Would you like to eat here or at the dining room?"

Mr. Wilson, startled, decides, "Oh yes... it's dinner time, isn't it? Sorry. My mind's a bit preoccupied...let's eat at the dining room."

He escorts the pregnant Margaret back. Their house is rather small, with only the dining area and the master bedroom. They're fortunate to have it, though, and the bonus gardening area too. There, Margaret likes to grow all kinds of plants including tomatoes, potatoes and a variety of roses — with some even specifically imported from other countries. For tonight's dinner, she uses fresh veggies from the makeshift garden. I can smell, as Mr. Wilson probably smells, his favorite dish: baked cheese and meat pasta. I'm sure it instantly delights his mood.

"Darling, how could I ever leave you with such amazing cooking?" he compliments. "Your cuisines are like shackles."

He finishes the pasta and shows approval by patting his stomach.

Margaret smiles, "As long as you like it, I don't mind cooking. Just don't make me do the dishes."

"I wouldn't bear asking you to wash dishes seeing how much energy you expend per day — especially with the pregnancy."

With this, I imagine Mr. Wilson collecting the dirty dishes and hand-washing them, calmly sliding each clean one into a rack. He goes to the balcony afterwards and resumes his previous reflection, sipping his fizzy drink. Margaret approaches him again and passively pries, "Darling, I know you're not supposed to speak about work details. But —"

"You're right," Mr. Wilson agrees. "Things are confidential." Then adds, "But let's say...in the hypothetical... it involves...a friend...or...someone we know..."

Margaret pauses for a moment then chimes, "Well, I feel that whether or not it's a friend, you must do what's right and arrest this person." When her husband doesn't respond she continues, "Is it one of your fellow officers?"

He shakes his head and takes her hand. She pats to comfort it, "You don't have to tell me — I'd understand that you'd get in trouble."

But he holds her hand firmer and I see Mrs. Wilson feeling the pain of his tighter grip.

"Honey," she whines. "You're hurting me."

He lets go, feeling guilty. This is the first time he caused his wife pain. "I'm sorry, darling," he apologies. "I'm just...overworked." He retakes her hand and gently kisses it, "I didn't mean it. Please accept my remorse."

She tells him it didn't hurt that much. Mr. Wilson finally opens, "Today, Commissioner McGrady gave each station's chief inspector a memo from the American consulate."

He pauses, not knowing if he should tell the next part. Margaret is silently curious. He finally continues, "It's from their Federal Bureau of Investigation. They say an American killer is hoping around the world, most likely in Mexico, Peru or Southeastern Asian countries like Thailand or Vietnam. But...they say the killer is especially likely in Hong Kong since his wife is from Hong Kong."

"Huh," thinks Margaret. "I couldn't think of anyone we'd know that'd fit such description."

"I initially thought the same," Mr. Wilson says. "But then I came up with someone."

"Who?"

"Well, like you, no one had came to mind until I learned the location of the murder — Texas."

Margaret's blue eyes widened.

"W-was it in Galveston?" she asks.

He nods.

"And you're thinking of arresting Johnny?" she gasps.

"I don't know," he sighs. "There's something I'd like to know before acting upon it."

"And what would that be?"

"The whole part about his wife being from Hong Kong."

"That's right," Margaret nods. "Jennifer's obviously Texan."

"Yes," nods Mr. Wilson. "That's what's been baffling me all day."

She consoles him. "Let's not worry too much until Sunday. We can pry then." She plants a kiss to show her support.

"You're right," her husband admits. "But please keep this between us. Any slip of this and it could endanger everyone."

"Sure," Margaret complies.

She drags his hand to their bedroom.

The following Sunday at church, I imagine Margaret seeking Jennifer and asking, "Oh darling, it's so good to see you. Hey, someone recently gave me the biggest piece of steak and I'd really like your advice on how to cook it. I hear barbequing is the best way — and the piece is just too large for James and I. We'd like someone to share it."

Laughing, Jennifer responds, "Well, I could show you how to do it. I *am* from Texas, after all. Haha! But no need to share it. We actually don't eat a lot of meat these days."

"But our grill isn't large enough," hints Margaret.

"Oh, that's no problem — you can borrow ours! Johnny hardly uses it. I can have him deliver it your home."

"It's not a bother, Jennifer! I want you two to come. To be honest, I get quite bored being all alone sometimes in the afternoons. It would be a good opportunity to know each other better."

Jennifer hesitates then replies, "It's a great idea, Margaret, really, but lately Johnny's not feeling too well these days, if you catch my drift."

Margaret nods and concedes, "Oh, in that case...I won't bother you both."

"I'm truly sorry. Next opportunity, Johnny and I will say yes."

The Wilsons go home disappointed.

Back home, I see Mr. Wilson contemplating the matter. He suddenly has a thought and dresses. Margaret feels a hunch and confronts him.

"I'm going to get a warrant from the station," he says matter-of-factly.

"Aren't you being a bit impulsive?" she asks. "The law

says to collect evidence, friends or not. Besides, it's not like they can easily escape Tai O. Let's take our time."

The next morning, Margaret gathers her purse and umbrella and makes her way to Johnny and Jennifer's home in the hills. It was typical for fog to appear in the spring time, but this autumn morning was full of it, perhaps because of the ocean breeze. She walks cautiously, careful not to slip from the grass dew. When she approaches the house, Jennifer opens the door and shows surprise to see Margaret. She invites her inside.

"I'm sorry I didn't tell you I'd come, Jennifer."

"It's alright. I've already woken."

"And where is Johnny?" asks Margaret. "Is he outside exercising?"

"Uh...no. H-he's in our bedroom resting."

"I know you told me not to bother you during this time, but I've got a matter to discuss. It's about childbirth."

"Oh!" Jennifer laughs in relief. "I...I mean, it's been forty years since I've reared children, but as a former nurse I'm sure I could help."

Happy with her answer, Margaret produces a bottle of pills. She pours four white tablets into her palm and explains, "I got these two days ago from the doctor. I'm hesitant to try them since I'm fearful of pharmaceuticals."

Jennifer takes the bottle and inquires, "Why not ask the doctor?"

Margaret blushes, "I actually got these from the pharmacy in his office. The doctor was busy then and I couldn't understand the pharmacist's English. I thought I'd come to you instead."

I imagine Jennifer taking the reading glasses from her neck and inspect the bottle.

"Dear, these are just common folic acid vitamins," she observes.

"Oh? — and what's their purpose?"

Jennifer puts down her glasses and explains, "It's for helping the baby's brain development. Although folic acid vitamins should've been given to you in the early stages of pregnancy. Why now?"

Margaret bites her lip.

"Welllll...the doctor hadn't mentioned I didn't need it back then. My folic acid count was high."

"Mmmph," agrees Jennifer. "Probably because you consume a lot of greens or fish. The locals don't use folic acid vitamins either — they're big on greens and fish. Animal waste too, from the intestines. If you can believe."

Margaret makes a face.

"I couldn't eat feces from intestines," she declares. "I wouldn't dare. What's the best greens for folic acid? I really don't want to take the pills."

"Spinach. Mustard greens — although the locals like to cook the mustard greens with ginger."

Margaret takes Jennifer's hand and pats it.

"Thank you, Jennifer. I wouldn't know what I'd do without you. I've learned a lot today."

Her sweet words softens the Texan. Jennifer suddenly has a thought and takes Margaret to the backyard.

"Careful of the slippery ground," she warns.

While the backyard is small, its view is magnificent. From its vantage point, rows of mountains can be seen. The sea wind is wonderful too; all of it reminds Margaret of England. So impressed was she with the scenery and Jennifer's garden that Margaret exclaims, "Oh, I absolutely love this place!"

"Me too," a gruff male voice chimes.

Mrs. Wilson looks back to find Johnny, in mere Polo pajamas, smiling at them. Jennifer immediately suggests, "It's cold, dear. Um, don't you think you oughta put on your favorite brown robe?"

Margaret apologizes, "I'm sorry. Our conversation must have awoken you, Johnny."

"Ah, hell," Johnny waves off. "I was already up. Just heard y'all's voices and thought I'd join in on the fun. *Heh.*"

Jennifer quickly takes some yam leaves from the garden and offers some to Margaret, "Here ya go. These yam leaves are high on folic acid."

Pleased, Margaret embraces her, "Jennifer, thank you so much. You remind me of my mother. So how exactly am I going to cook these yam leaves?"

"Oh, well, we just cook it like the Chinese. Simply add garlic and lots of oil."

"Mmm," nods Margaret. "Well, you've certainly got habits of the local culture down."

As they speak, a neighborhood boy passes by the backyard fence and casually tosses over a banana peel. Jennifer shows her displeasure by berating him in native Cantonese.

Impressed, Mrs. Wilson remarks, "Wow! For a transplant, your Cantonese is certainly impressive. Hope mine will be as good as yours in a few years."

"Ha!" Jennifer scoffs. "Well, I was born here in 1877. Lived in Hong Kong up until I met Johnny." She pats the shocked Mrs. Wilson. "Not everyone from Hong Kong is ethnically Chinese, you know."

Her laugh pierces Mrs. Wilson's heart as they make a few last bits of conversation. Mrs. Wilson then fights off tears on her way home. Once there, she lets them pour. Her husband, startled, doesn't know what to do. She sits on the sofa with a daze similar to the one Mr. Wilson had the previous night. He sits adjacent to her, listening.

"When you mentioned that the murderer's wife was born in Hong Kong," Margaret whispers. "It didn't occur to us that not everyone born here is ethnically Chinese."

Mr. Wilson's eyes light up.

"That's true," he realizes. "Just as our child will be from Hong Kong. Damn it, how could I've been so dense?"

"Jennifer told me her father was Italian. He moved here as part of a clergy, bringing the whole family to Hong Kong."

"So how did she meet Johnny?" Mr. Wilson interrupts. "That might help with the investigation."

"Do you recall hearing about a plague here, back around 1890? Ten thousand people died — "

"So how did she meet Johnny?" impatiently repeats her husband.

"Will you please let me explain?!"

"...okay."

Margaret stares at him, then resumes.

"Jennifer told me she was a nurse at Tung Wah hospital during the plague. Johnny was a seafarer, stopping by Hong

Kong. On the last night that his crew left for shore, he got very drunk, relieved himself in a dark alleyway and was bitten by a rat. Thinking nothing of it, he got on board the ship only to be deemed infected by the captain. The crew left him at Tung Wah hospital as they sailed off. As the only foreign-looking nurse there, Jennifer was assigned to Johnny — that's how they met and fell in love."

"Ah," nods Mr. Wilson. "I see now."

The next day, after lunch, I imagine the Wilsons bringing whiskey to the suspects' front door. Johnny is surprised to see them and he invites them inside. They glance and see Jennifer washing dishes in the kitchen, unaware of their visit. Although Margaret had spent some time here the previous morning, it was mostly at their backyard. She lets the two men converse and casually approaches the kitchen.

"Margaret!" yelps out Jennifer. She stops her chores. "I-I don't mind you visiting, but I'd really prefer you end these unannounced stopovers."

Mrs. Wilson blushes.

"I'm sorry, Jennifer," she says. "It's just that when James heard how warmly you received me yesterday, he just thought he should come over too and say thank you. We brought whiskey."

Not satisfied with this answer, Jennifer glances at Johnny in the living room and loudly proclaims, "Well, Johnny's still sick. He can't be bothered."

She dries her hands with a towel.

"Oh honey, let them stay longer," Johnny laughs. "Certainly they're here for a reason, right?"

"No, Johnny. The doctors said you need to rest. Remember?"

"I got the energy, dammit!" he shouts back.

Seeing how there was no way she can get the two to leave, Jennifer goes back to her dishwashing. Margaret senses the deep animosity and joins her husband. After awhile,

Jennifer loses her temper and storms into the living room. When she sees what they're drinking she shouts, "Oh you devil Brits, you're quite something, aren't you? Giving a sick man alcohol! The nerve! There's a special place in hell for you! Your presence isn't welcomed here anymore — I'm asking you to leave!"

The Wilsons begin to do so, but Johnny summons them back down.

"Now Jennifer!" he asserts. "Drinking the whiskey was my idea! Come, James and Margaret, let's drink up."

Angered by her husband's defiance, Jennifer starts storming upstairs, then, as a second thought, returns and takes the bottle away. As they watch her leave, it takes Margaret and James all their courage to continue their mission, feeling terrible that it was their first time causing a scene.

"So...um, Johnny," leads Mr. Wilson. "Any stories about your time in Texas?"

Johnny swirls his glass.

"Umph," he shrugs. "Yes, I've mostly lived in south Texas. There was a murder that took place."

The answer shocks the Wilsons.

Suddenly, Jennifer storms back and grabs Margaret's handbag, flinging it onto her lap.

"Enough!" she shuts up Johnny. "My husband needs his rest, you two have to leave. Immediately!"

But Johnny calms her.

"Come on, dear, the cat's out the bag," he scoffs. "Can't you see? Shucks." He calmly looks at the chief inspector, "I know why you came, young man — and I want you to know, I'm gonna be very cooperative. "

Mr. Wilson clears his throat.

"Well, if we're gonna be frank here, Johnny, why don't you tell us what really happened?"

Jennifer eases from her protective scowl.

"Sigh," she says. "Might as well face the music then. We're tired of running."

"Yes," agreed the chief inspector. "Best to be honest."

As Johnny begins to speak, he suddenly goes into a

harsh bout of coughing. His wife rushes to pat him while Margaret fetches a warm glass of water from the kitchen. Johnny slowly takes the glass and recovers.

Jennifer speaks for him, "I'd say if we're going to speak of this, it's best to start when Johnny and I moved to Texas." She pauses to collect her thoughts. "We lived on his grandfather's farm. It was large with cattle and sheep and there's a cemetery where his grandparents and relatives are buried. The farm land interferes with the construction of two large roads and the state is forced to build around it. Our kids grew up happy there. The crops were more than enough to feed us. Then, five years ago, some fancy oil company joined forces with Galveston's mayor and started offering lowball deals for our land."

Here, Johnny joins, "That damn Terry. Slippery Terry, we'd call him. I knew him all the way back from high school. Teammates in football. Never amounted to much in academics, but the guy sure had talking smarts. Talked his way into becoming mayor eventually." Johnny sighs and softens his tone. "I suppose looking back now, I should've handled it calmer. We wouldn't have been in this mess if it weren't for my temper."

"Certainly if I'd been there," Jennifer adds. "I definitely wouldn't have let things escalate."

Mr. Wilson considers their words, then asks, "Where'd you go right after the murder? Was it Hong Kong?"

"We...," Johnny pauses. "We drove to Mexico immediately after the murder."

"But isn't it far to the border?" Margaret asks. "I mean, I know it's a neighboring country to the United States..."

"It's only a couple of hours from Texas," Jennifer assures. "Quick enough to get through before the feds noticed."

The tension fades considerably and the four of them calmly sit. Jennifer hastily makes Johnny tea.

"We know just being in Mexico would make us an easy target for the FBI. Fortunately, as a seaman, I knew of ways to get us out through Lima, Peru."

He sips his tea, though from its prompt creation, its leaves float on the surface and much of it clings to his mouth.

The image of his mouth being full of tea leaves spawns some much needed laughter that cools the tension.

Mr. Wilson calmly asks, "How did you get through Hong Kong customs? Certainly you weren't using your real passports."

"We've had falsified identities since Mexico," Johnny calmly replies.

"So your real names aren't Johnny and Jennifer then," muses Margaret.

"Names are merely labels," Jennifer shrugs. "We call the local dog Yellow, for instance. We've no idea its real name."

"Yellow?" asks Margaret.

"In America, we have these flying insects called Yellow Jackets," explains Johnny. "The dog was always following me around like a Yellow Jacket — ready to bite my ass off any given time."

They chuckle. Johnny offers his hands and submits, "You can now have me, chief inspector. I'm ready."

Mr. Wilson gently pats Johnny's hand, "I actually didn't bring my handcuffs."

The Wilsons bid their goodbyes, leaving Jennifer a kiss.

"We'll be at the station by nine in the morning," assures Jennifer.

From a distance, they see the sun setting. As night falls, the two lay awake in their bed at ten. Tossing and turning, the chief inspector gets the curiosity of his wife who asks him, "How come you didn't arrest them today, James?"

"Well, I figured if they'd voluntarily turned themselves in it'd go well with the American juries and maybe even reduce his sentences."

"But...aren't you afraid they'd flee?"

Mr. Wilson clasps his wife's hand.

"Honey, I trust him," he whispers.

Margaret leans on his shoulder, "Me too."

Chapter 8

By eight the next morning, the chief inspector arrives at work. I imagine him calmly sitting at his desk, checking the FBI briefing one final time. Everything about Johnny and Jennifer's story matches the details. Yet, as the clock ticks closer to nine, Mr. Wilson grows nervous as evidenced by his sweaty palms. The large wall clock finally chimes and he patiently sits. By the tenth chime, he loses his composure and grabs his gun and belt, heading towards the house up the hill.

He finds the front gate shut and no answer to his repeated knockings. The chief inspector paces around Johnny and Jennifer's home, peering through the windows until he finds one ajar near the backyard. From there, he lets himself into the house and immediately walks upstairs to the master bedroom. There, Mr. Wilson finds a mess; clothes and items are everywhere. He plants an angry punch to the wall, embarrassed he'd been so merciful the previous day — a warrant for their arrest is in order.

However, as he storms outside, he gets a glimpse of a neighbor and casually asks if she knows of the couple's whereabouts.

"Well," the neighbor speaks in fast Cantonese, "around five this morning, I woke up to ambulance lights. Someone from that residence must've dialed 999. I looked out the window and saw the old American gentleman being taken by a stretcher."

Mr. Wilson summons his best Cantonese, "And...the...American...woman?"

The neighbor gives a bewildered look before decrying, "Come on now, did you really think she'd leave her husband's side and flee back to America?"

Word brakes that Johnny passed away before the ambulance arrive at the hospital. Margaret receives the news from her husband and makes a trip to console Jennifer. She finds her sitting in an empty hospital bed holding Johnnie's old walking stick. Margaret lets her tears fall.

"Now, now," scorns Jennifer. "Don't cry, my dear. It's not good for the baby. This was probably the best for Johnny anyway, leaving Earth in my arms."

Margaret dries her eyes, "So what are you going to do now?"

"Well, I've already talked to your husband and had the death certificate done. All that's left is to bury Johnny in our farm's cemetery."

A few days later, a simple funeral is attended by Father Gordon and the members of their church, including the Wilsons.

Jennifer's past is kept under wraps.

A week goes by and the Wilsons escort Jennifer to the airport. There, they see her through the outside gate, watching her go into the shuttle bus that connects to an awaiting Pan-Am. Margaret can't bear to say goodbye and she's comforted by her husband, who wraps his coat around her from the strong breeze. Across the runway, they see a black coffin being placed into the cargo hold. The Wilsons watch from the runway until the propellers of the Pan-Am spin. Soon the plane is a tiny blue speck in the sky.

I figure due to their sleeplessness and distress, the Wilsons easily get sea sick from the ferry ride back to Tai O. Feeling an uneasiness she's never felt before, Margaret abruptly aims for the sea and vomits. Her husband rushes to her side, unsure of what to do. Relief comes as she notifies she's okay and a caring seaman approach her with Tiger Balm. Though she refuses to rub herself with it due to the smell, another seaman offers some dried salted plums, which she plops into her mouth and they calm her.

When they arrive home, she tells Mr. Wilson, "Love, I feel a bit discomfort. Be a dear and wait a bit before I can cook for us."

But her husband immediately suggests, "You mustn't strain yourself. Tonight's dinner is directly under my responsibility."

He tucks his wife into bed, kisses her head and decides

that fried chicken is the easiest thing to cook. After taking a handful of drumsticks from the freezer, he plops them into a tub of water and waits a few hours. As time goes by, he is surprised to find them still frozen. He feels Margaret embrace him from the back and chuckle.

"Big Chef," she teases. "Is your lover's meal ready?"

"Hate to disappoint you," he observes a frozen drumstick. "But I think we're gonna have to order out."

"Sure. No deliveries. Let's go the plaza area."

Pleased with her idea, Mr. Wilson immediately changes clothes.

"Ah," he remembers midway to the plaza. "I forgot the French cuisine place we usually frequent is closed tonight. We'd have to settle for local food."

"Not a problem," shrugs Margaret. "I haven't had Chinese in awhile."

I imagine Mr. Wilson frowning at this, unhappy with the thought.

"I wouldn't know how to order," he adds. "None of their menus are in English."

"Well, if you don't want anything local, what do you want then?"

Suddenly, a high-pitched voice shouts, "Chief Inspector! I.......happy....... to see you and.......wife here!"

They turn to face a familiar dark-skinned and thin girl. Her smile reveals two large dimples.

"Judy!" remarks Margaret.

"I...think...you...forgot...me!" she continues smiling. "You...after-dinner...walk?"

She makes finger gestures of strolling.

"Oh!" Margaret laughs dismissively. "You might not believe this, but James and I are actually indecisive as to where we'd eat."

Judy takes awhile to sink in their English, then finally comprehends and suggests, "Ah...you...how about...join my house? We...eh...have...meat...vegetables...my father, today he catch...big fish..."

"We don't mean to be a bother," politely declines Mr. Wilson. "Plus, there are probably a lot of people at your house already."

"No...no! Just me...and...my brothers and sisters."

Margaret tilts her head. "Well, what happened to your step-mother and step-brother?"

"*Dead fat po* in banquet...father...still fishing...you come, ok? Tonight...me and...brothers...sisters...only."

Margaret agrees over Mr. Wilson's hesitation. She is excited at the idea of visiting her first Chinese household. When they enter the now-familiar makeshift sheet metal house, I imagine the siblings cowering and hiding at the presence of the two foreigners. Margaret politely observes Judy plopping the fresh ingredients in the rusty sink and prepare for cooking. The kitchen is very small and packed.

"Do you need help?" Margaret offers.

Judy fervently waves her away. "I...okay...can cook myself...do it since childhood. Small people number...okay...can handle..."

Margaret observes her awhile, leaning on the wooden kitchen door.

She muses, "That's quite a lot there for so few people. Are you sure no one else is coming?"

"Just...side dishes," Judy dismisses. "And boyfriend William...he come later."

Margaret suppresses further questioning, seeing how Judy is already overworked in the intense heat — even the poor girl's hair is drenched with sweat. She watches as Judy pours a bowl of water into an iron wok and as the water boils, Judy multi-tasks and washes some raw rice. Afterwards, the raw rice is poured into a pan that's being heated from a ground brick stove and while this is happening, Judy minces pork and mui choy with a cleaver. She then places the minced mix into the cooking rice and attends to the wok as she steams fish and ginger within the now-intensely boiling water. She puts a lid over them and begins washing vegetables. All of this is done with impressive fluidity.

Seeing how the kitchen area is devoid of ventilation, Mr. Wilson stops his picture gazing and pulls his wife out, fearing the kitchen smoke might harm her pregnancy. Margaret peaks behind a curtain of a small room and sees Judy's little brothers doing homework. Their area is packed with a lone bunk bed. The Wilsons convince the children to come out of the dim lighting and into the brighter dining room. There, they notice the homework is English and Mr. Wilson teases its simplicity. Margaret breaks the ice by tutoring them.

After dinner, the Wilsons merrily make their way back home with Margaret bragging about her teaching skills. Her husband, however, contemplates a deeper topic — how to help Judy with her own living quarters.

The next night, the Wilsons can finally attend their favorite French restaurant in Tai O. Mrs. Wilson orders a rack of lamb along with French Onion soup. Her husband also orders French Onion soup to go with his steak medium-well. Drinking his soup, Mr. Wilson chimes, "Dearest, I feel that our unborn child has given us many blessings."

With a sullen heart, Margaret replies, "Not everything has been a blessing. You've done many good deeds, but...we've lost two good friends..."

Mr. Wilson puts down his spoon and holds her hand.

"I still can't believe it happened," he sighs.

Suddenly, Margaret lets out a yelp which sends her husband rushing to her side.

"It's quite alright, love," she calms him. "Just our little angel kicking, that's all."

Mr. Wilson doesn't quite believe she's completely alright.

"Are you completely sure nothing is bothering you?"

"Well," admits Margaret. "Jennifer was supposed to be there for me...for advice on the baby. Now that she's gone...I fear I've lost an ally."

"Don't worry. Our obstetrician recommended us a very nice hospital. Tsang Yuk is the best maternity ward in the city."

"I know, James. I know. Best medical staff and all that..."

"And there's me, your loving husband."

Margaret glares at him. "Beyond the moral support, I mean. I'd need someone to take care of the baby with me.

Besides, with your all-important job as the chief inspector — you'd hardly have the time."

"I think I have someone in mind..."

"Who, James? Don't tell me it's one of the locals. I need to be able to communicate. I —"

"Judy," her husband smiles. "I was referring to Judy. Her English is passable."

"She's younger than me, James. How can someone who's never had children possible be considered experienced?"

"I'm just saying, dear. She knows English and maybe —"

"And maybe what? You don't seem to understand the gravity of the situation, do you? It's absolutely important that I'm able to properly communicate with the help and —"

A waiter comes and interrupts their conversation. Their main course is placed in front of them as they stare at each other in silence.

"You were saying...?" Mr. Wilson resumes.

"Never the bloody mind!" dismisses his wife.

They finish their meal without further incident.

I imagine the next few days, Mr. Wilson fervently seeking a suitable helper for Margaret in Tai O. Unfortunately, any local woman capable of speaking English had long since found a cozy job with a foreign business; everyone else spoke little to no English. Eventually, he gives in to the doctors' advice and moves his wife to the inner city, where she'd be closer to the English-speaking hospital staff. Not less than a day afterwards, he finds a capable helper in the inner city, a self-proclaimed Polish woman called Marie. This gives Mr. Wilson some peace of mind until Margaret calls him three days later.

"Mary is gone," she says. "Can you either help find someone or be with me? The baby's about to be born."

"Can't the hospital let you in a few days early? I don't mind paying extra."

He hears a deep, annoyed sigh from the other side of the phone.

"If only you knew how many hundreds of pregnant women are waiting everyday at Tsang Yuk. Even foreign-born government families like us have to wait, even if we're promised highest priority."

"I see," breathes Mr. Wilson. "So why did Marie leave?"

"Didn't you hear? She lied to us, James. I could detect that accent a mile away. She's German...and not just German, she and her husband are ex-Nazi's."

A pause comes.

"Ex-Nazis," Mr. Wilson mutters. "That was very astute of you, darling. Those damn bloody Germans! I can still hear those air raid sirens since I was fourteen. Running toward the bomb shelters, shoes half on."

He hears a slight sniffling from the other line.

"You okay, dearest?"

"Pardon," she dismisses. "Just the memories. My uncle, who took care of me after my parents died from the war, got killed by their bombing."

"Ten years and it still haunts you," nods Mr. Wilson. "Well, I'm heading to the city right now, okay? Don't you worry your pretty little head."

Putting down the phone, the chief inspector sighs at the large piles of work that needs to be done and decides to regulate it to his subordinates.

His wife needs him.

When he arrives to the inner city, Margaret casually suggests, "There was someone from the pile of applications that seemed suitable. A retired music teacher."

"Mmm, yes. Mrs. McCourt from Scotland, was it?"

"You remember."

"I interviewed her, darling. Didn't think she'd be right for you."

"Why not, James?"

"It said in her application she was 63. Well, in person she looked about 73. Face full of wrinkles...but that wasn't the main reason. The reason was because she could hardly walk and by the hospital there're some pretty steep slopes."

"Heh," Margaret shrugs. "I guess the help is *you* then."

Mr. Wilson sighs, "I'm afraid you're going to be disappointed in this also, dear. Smuggling checks have increased of late. Commissioner McGrady wants me to be very active on them."

"Why now?"

"The Communists have joined with North Korea in their recent war. There's a tight embargo in China, so they're using Hong Kong as an entry point for prohibited goods — I'm sorry, I really can't skip work."

Margaret frowns, "Well, what do we do?"

"I can visit as often as possible."

She leans on him and puts her head next to his chest.

"*Sigh*. What about Judy then?" Margaret asks. "Is she still available?"

"Mmm...don't you dislike her?"

"I didn't say I *disliked* her, James. I just thought she's inexperienced."

"Well," smiles Mr. Wilson. "She's raised her siblings on her own. I think she can do it. Besides, even if she turns out to be a mediocre child taker, she can still be useful with laundry and cleaning the house."

His wife looks up and gives him a look of admiration.

"James Wilson," she declares. "With that convincing tongue, if you weren't already a police officer you'd be an excellent salesman." She nods. "Judy it is then. Just make sure she doesn't live with us."

"Not a problem, " he kisses her head. "There isn't an extra room in our house anyway."

Chapter 9

Early Christmas Morning, despite the numerous parties he could've attended the prior evening, Mr. Wilson stays with Margaret for the birth of their beautiful child. They name her Lucy, a name which means 'born at dawn'. As Judy attends to Margaret, Mr. Wilson is present the entire day. After they're discharged a half-week later, Margaret is seen carrying the baby in protective blankets, fearful of the blistering cold weather. Behind her is Judy, carrying the rest of Mrs. Wilson's clothes. The newborn cries, not comfortable in her mother's arms.

When their taxi arrives at the pier, Judy volunteers to momentarily carry Lucy, a gesture the tired Margaret appreciates. The baby sleeps soundly in Judy's arms during the ferry ride to Tai O. As Margaret lays her head in the chief inspector's shoulder, he turns over to Judy and gives her a thumbs up.

At the Wilsons' home, Judy gently delivers baby Lucy into her new crib. Margaret, tired and lying in bed, occasionally reaches to the crib and smiles at her new daughter.

"Thank you, Judy," she whispers.

Judy, whose English has improved thanks to Margaret, expresses, "You're welcome, Mrs. Wilson."

They share a laugh of gratitude.

Not long after Judy leaves, the chief inspector is at a loss of what to make for his wife in the kitchen. The doorbell rings and Mr. Wilson is surprised to find Judy back with Chinese groceries. She's too immersed in her preparation for him to thank her and he merely observes, watching her set aside ginger, dates, fungus, black beans and chicken. With the strong addition of rice wine, whatever Judy produces creates a wonderful aroma and it gives Mr. Wilson absolute faith in his new maid.

"Although...I...no child," Judy explains while cooking. "I see...*dead fat po*...make this soup...when pregnant. It...good for...restoring...blood...after birth."

"That's quite common sense logic," admires a voice.

They both turn and see Margaret standing, quietly observing them.

"When I was at the hospital," Margaret continues. "I had plenty of conversations with the staff there. You know, the Orientals' medical methods aren't too different from ours in England. Thank you once again Judy."

Judy politely smiles, "It is...my duty."

"We apologize for your low salary," Mr. Wilson apologizes. "We'll pay more when we can."

"It's...okay. Enough...to support...my family. Also...Mrs. Wilson...she teach me English."

Margaret smiles, "You're always welcome to teach me Cantonese, Judy."

Mr. Wilson's laughter wakes up the baby. As Margaret attends to put Lucy back to sleep, Judy finishes the dishes. Mr. Wilson, working on his files, sees Judy leaving afterwards and follows her to the door. The weather is now colder than it was at noon, so he runs to the master room and grabs his wife's spare coat.

"Oh no, no!" Judy refuses, clutching her thin blue jacket. "This...jacket I have already...it's...warm...enough."

He watches her leave until she's faded into the harsh winter landscape. Back inside, he takes a look at Lucy whose face is so red and crisp like a ripe tomato. She has just finished her milk. He picks his daughter up and lifts her closer to him, applying a kiss with his prickly beard. Lucy cries in pain and Margaret laughs, rubbing her smooth face to Lucy's cheek. She puts her back to her crib.

Her husband kisses her and remarks, "That's our baby, darling."

Three nights later, the chief inspector is skimming through his usual paperwork in the living room while Judy washes the dishes. The maid yawns a few times, prompting him to remark, "You seem tired. Had trouble sleeping?"

Judy blushes and replies, "Last night...neighbor Gang and two sons...setting up for fish...they do not stop...until five...this morning."

"Hmmm...and this happens every night?"

"No. Just...two...or three...per week," Judy pauses. "But so funny...usually...Gang and sons...they lazy. Usually wake up last. Prepare late, come back...earliest of fisherman."

"They must be good at fishing then."

"*Hunh*!" scoffs Judy. "They are...terrible fisherman, Mr. Wilson! No patience!...when I small girl, fish with father...they always give up, go home...my father...me...we just switch spot. Always we catch fish this way."

"Then Gang and his two sons must not make a lot of money."

Judy dries off the last dish.

"Yes, Mr. Wilson...even when their...net break...they ask my father...to fix. Do not...even try to fix...themself. They lazy!"

"So how're they doing now?"

"Hmm. It funny...suspicious... they leave partnership with my father...but now they look like more rich. Even...have...a radio." She slowly heads towards the door. "Mr. Wilson, I finish now...I go home."

Mr. Wilson attempts to give her his wife's coat.

"It's really cold out there, Judy. Please take this. I don't want you catching a cold."

"Do not worry...short distance...tonight I live in boyfriend William's house." Realizing how it must sound she clarifies, "I sleep with his sister. Nothing more."

"Oh, no...it's not what I'm thinking. And even if it is, my wife and I stayed together before marriage. It's no big deal. I won't judge."

"You and Mrs. Wilson...foreigners. For you, okay. But...Chinese...we are conservative. We cannot do that."

The chief inspector smiles, "I'm just teasing you, Judy. But now you've got me curious about this Gang and this two sons. Do you mind if you can take me to where he lives?"

Judy nods, "Of course, Mr. Wilson."

He goes to his room and tells his wife his planned reconnaissance.

"I'm going with Judy to check something out," he informs.

Margaret calls out to him, but he's already left.

When he returns, the chief inspector finds Margaret holding Lucy in the middle of the living room, heating herself near the fireplace. The lone illumination reveals her displeasure and Mr. Wilson remarks, "You're awake. Did the baby wake you?"

"Why'd you go out?" she ignores his question. "Was it really because you wanted to walk her home?"

"Who — Judy?" he laughs. "You're being absurd, dearest."

Margaret immediately gets up to show her seriousness.

"You think I'm humoring you, do you James? Why hesitate and think when I question you?"

Margaret's interrogative nature sends him to a state of confusion. His lack of response further infuriates her and she heads toward the bedroom with Lucy. Mr. Wilson stops her and explains, "I-I can't tell you exactly why I went tonight. But you got to trust me. It's part of police work."

"So why bring Judy into it? Why didn't you just go alone, hmm?"

"Because I was talking to her earlier and she mentioned a suspicious neighbor. I connected the dots. I believe they're part of a contraband network. She knows where they live. I can't tell you anymore details, Margaret — you've got to trust me."

"So why not send your men to investigate tomorrow? Just get the address down from Judy!"

Mr. Wilson sighs, "Look, I saw something tonight at the suspect's home, okay? There was a game of mah-jong inside."

"And how does this relate to your immediate investigation?"

"Two of the mah-jong players were my own officers, Margaret. These men were loaded. Money and contraband were everywhere. I've just discovered two corrupt officers in my unit. That's what I saw."

His wife paused.

"I see — so, what're you going to do?"

"I'll set up a meeting with the commissioner tomorrow. Get his idea about how to do this."

Apologetic, I see Margaret's face soften. She comes to her husband and offers a repentant kiss.

"You know I love you, James. Be careful."

He nods and takes her to their room, embracing her as she hushes the child to sleep.

"Just out of curiosity," he whispers. "What aroused your jealousy anyway?"

Margaret stares at him, "If you really think I'd be jealous over some fisherman's daughter, you really don't know me. I lack faith in you — that's what it's really about."

"When have I give you a reason distrust me?"

She coldly walks past him, places Lucy in her crib and rests in bed. Mr. Wilson calmly attempts to caress her, sliding a hand up her waist, then onto her breast. She immediately swats him.

"Come on," huffs her husband. "It's been awhile, Margaret."

"Doctor's orders. He strictly said no sex so soon after

childbirth."

The chief inspector backs off her, "I see, then. You're threatened by a skinny, dark-skinned peasant because you know if I truly wanted it, I could get that kind of attention from her."

Margaret glares, "Are you an untamed beast or a person?"

Her husband sneers and walks out, only to be stopped by her.

"Come on James, if you want, we can do it tonight. But please be gentle."

And with this, he hops onto bed and embraces Margaret.

At midnight a week later, the chief inspector and a handful of officers do a stakeout near the neighborhood of Gang and his two sons. The officers are stuffed in layers of clothing with scarves heavily covering their faces. Being used to freezing temperatures in England, Mr. Wilson needs no such attire and stands defiantly in the cold wintery weather. He patiently observes with binoculars at the mah-jong game taking place inside Gang's makeshift home. The strong sea breeze violently shakes the sheet metal, though none of the noise appears to disturb the men's attention. Mah-jong tile after mah-jong tile click and clack.

One of the players is Officer Wah Chai.

From a nearby alley, the stakeout team sees an old pickup truck approaching. As it stops in front of Gang's house, the driver and two men cuts the engine and begins to unload a dozen boxes at the door. They knock, interrupting the mah-jong game. The door eventually opens and the smuggled goods seep inside Gang's home. As the business is finished, the three men calmly walk back into the truck and start the engine. Immediately, the chief inspector takes out his walkie-talkie and orders the Mui Wo unit to intercept the leaving truck. As Gang and his two sons load the contraband into a motorboat, Mr. Wilson orders a pair of his men to arrest Wah Chai, who is leaving from the front door.

"Whatever you do," he instructs with his best Chinese, "don't take him to our bloody Tai O station. We don't want to risk corrupt officers freeing him. Lock Wai Chai in the main police headquarters instead."

"Yes, sir," nods the arresting team.

No sooner than ten minutes, Gang and his sons take off but are chased back to shore by incoming police boats. Mr. Wilson arrests them. A quick search of their boat reveals mostly penicillin and other medical supplies.

Early the next morning, the chief inspector wakes up in a cheery mood, kissing his wife as she breast feeds Lucy. At the sight of her plump, beautiful body he can't resist and takes her hand, whispering, "The operation was a success last night."

They make love again.

At the main headquarters' interrogation room, Mr. Wilson enters and sits adjacent to Wah Chai. He thumbs through the interview transcripts then glares at his former colleague.

"You've got to believe me, boss," pleads Wah Chai. "I wasn't involved with the smuggling ring."

The chief inspector slams the pile of transcripts on the interrogation desk.

"Aside from the part you were playing mah-jong," he asserts in his best Cantonese. "Everything else you said are A LIE."

Panic stricken, Wah Chai begs, "Y-you got to believe me, boss. It's true...all of it!"

I imagine Mr. Wilson irritated, fully knowing the character of Wah Chai.

"So you're telling me, Wai Chai, that you knew nothing about Gang and his two sons?"

The former officer shifts his eyes, sending the chief inspector to pound his fist in rage.

"You were a part of Her Majesty's police!" Mr. Wilson cries. "You know full well to report anything illegal to me, your superior!"

Wai Chai looks down.

"But —"

"But what, Wai Chai?!"

The corrupt officer defiantly stares up, fueled by conviction.

"You're an Englishman, boss" he bites back. "How would you truly understand how the people here feel? Just because I wear a British uniform, I'm still akin to loving my own people. How can I stand ideal knowing thousands in China are dying from sickness? The contraband are the only way to save them!"

Mr. Wilson bites his lip. Not wanting to get too political, he changes topics, "So how do you know Gang anyway?"

"His sons and I are childhood friends. We're close as brothers. I've told them many times to stay out of the smuggling life. But...I had a relative recently that fought with the Communists. He died due to a shortage in medical treatments. After that happened, I saw no harm in what Gang was doing."

Softening his tone, the chief inspector empathizes, "Just tell me, Wah Chai. I've known you long enough. Was there anything...personally beneficial in your involvement with Gang?"

"N-no sir...you have to believe me. It was all under good intentions."

Mr. Wilson walks up to his long time colleague and sighs, "I believe your heart now. I do. But you know that in court, it'll be Gang's words against yours."

"Yeah — I know."

The chief inspector leaves the interrogation room.

After months in court, Gang and his son are found guilty. Wah Chai is also found guilty but with a reduced sentence thanks to his indirect involvement and a letter of recommendation from Mr. Wilson. Wah Chai loses his job and all benefits associated.

Chapter 10

To celebrate Mr. Wilson's new promotion as Commander of the Lantau Island Police Force, all the island's agencies gather for dinner at the area's biggest seafood restaurant one rainy spring evening. At the center of their attention is Lucy, whose take on her father's blue eyes and mother's fair skin has her admirers mesmerized. Beside the Wilsons sits Judy, the main caretaker for the beautiful baby. Judy's boyfriend is also there, standing awkwardly among strangers. He notices a look of admiration she has for Mr. Wilson.

As their meals are ready, the guests dissipate from the baby and gather to their seating. Not long afterwards, the door opens and a familiar face makes his way into the restaurant, body soaking from the evening drizzle. He folds his umbrella and places it into a nearby rack.

"Wai Chai!" one of the officers have the nerve to call out. "Come and have a drink with myself and the new commander!"

Awkwardly, the disgraced former officer walks towards Mr. Wilson and shakes his hand.

"Congratulations, Commander," nods Wai Chai. "Thanks to your letter, I was quickly paroled."

The new commander gives Wai Chai an affectionate pat to the back.

"All water under the bridge," he smiles. "Don't let your emotions get the best of you anymore."

A Tai O associate suddenly approaches with two glasses of wine.

"A toast to the new commander!" orders the associate.

Both men take a glass and Mr. Wilson prepares a speech with his best Cantonese.

"Tonight, I feel joy. To be around you and to see Wai Chai free from prison. The other reason, of course, is the recent news that Margaret and I are expecting another baby."

A growing applause consumes the banquet. One-by-one the guests gather around and congratulate them. They offer toast after toast, filling the new commander's glass as fast as he can finish it.

"The character 'son' and 'daughter', when combined, make the character for 'good'," flatters an officer. "In Chinese, this is a great combination for children. One boy, one girl — my most heartfelt wises, Commander."

More drinks are poured and soon Margaret and Judy attempt to stop the toasting. Their efforts, however, were deficient in stopping the congratulatory onslaught. I imagine Mr. Wilson's laughter growing in volume and afterwards, being carried home by both Judy and her boyfriend William. At the front door of the commander's home, Mr. Wilson lunges at William and vomits all over his clothes. Margaret lets them in the house while carrying a screaming Lucy. The baby's crying drowns the other noises in the living room. I imagine William excusing himself, washing off the vomit in the W.C. as Judy carries the giant Mr. Wilson into his bedroom.

As she gently places him in bed, she feels a tight grip on her, preventing her from leaving. Judy, panicking, attempts to pull away, but the new commander applies greater force to pin her. The maid's screams are uncompetitive against the wails of Lucy and slowly, Mr. Wilson mounts her, ripping away her clothes. He breaks into a boorish smile and undoes his belt as minutes pass and he finally dismounts her, satisfied with his demeritorious action. When his senses recover, a somewhat sober Mr. Wilson finds himself lying on his bedroom floor, a few feet from him is a naked Judy cowering in bloodstained bed sheets, crying. Before a wave of remorse takes him, he hears the tirade of his daughter's screams louder and closer as the bedroom door opens to its entirety and Margaret gasping, horrified at the scandalous spectacle. She uses her free arm to repeatedly punch Mr. Wilson, knocking him senseless as the drunkard comprehends the assault. He makes out fragments of cursing and blaspheme.

William, late in discovering the incidence, quickly comes to aid the terrorized Judy. He quickly gives his coat and carries her.

"Don't be afraid," he calms her. "I'm going to send for a doctor and report this beast to the police. They'll lock this monster away."

Margaret accompanies them, leaving both Lucy and the beaten Mr. Wilson in their home.

At the hospital, Margaret deliberately seeks out a Welsh doctor and fibs, "The boyfriend...he was too rough on her." Then, taking William aside, exclaims in English, "I know you and Judy are affected, but think how I feel as the wife too. Think of how any negativity on James will affect our well-being."

William softens his demeanor.

"I know what happened was horrible, William. And I'm asking you to forgive James...to...to consider any reparations from our end. We can give you both money...and Judy, I hear she dreams of becoming an artist. I personally know the director of the London Academy of Arts. I could give her a letter of recommendation, have Judy go to school in England. We'll even cover the airfare."

The young man thinks it over, shaking his head.

"No, Mrs. Wilson," he answers in English. "If I take your offer, it would be an insult to the situation — as well as a victory for the British."

"Yes...you see? My husband and I are British. How could you entertain the idea of speaking poorly of a Commander? No judge would throw the book on James. You and I both know this."

William defiantly tilts his head.

"I believe that justice will be done," he nods.

Sternness fills Margaret's expression.

"And how could you properly testify when you weren't witnessing it. Were you there at the exact moment, William? Did you actually hear Judy's pleads for help? I was the first witness. All I saw was consent. Adulterous, unchaste consent — who do you think the court will believe, the testimony of a noble Englishwoman...or the uncouth words of a blundering Chinaman?"

After a short pause, he stares at the ground, slowly accepting the grim reality.

"The art school tuition," he softly concedes. "Is it expensive?"

"Don't worry about tuition. The scholarship will cover it, provided Judy is in good academic standing and behavior. We might not have a lot of money now, but with James' promotion, we'll cover your cost of living in England."

William continues staring at the ground, then boldly declare, "Okay, Mrs. Wilson. I'll accept the scholarship. But know this...I'm only taking Judy to England to get away from this pain. We won't take your money; it symbolizes compliance. You can keep that dirty filth."

The Englishwoman nods, feeling ashamed to have resorted to bribery. Nevertheless, she hopes William will successfully persuade Judy to move.

After the hospital, Margaret returns to her home to find Mr. Wilson slumping on the sofa, hands on his head. Without looking at him, she heads to Lucy's crib to find the baby peacefully sleeping. Her husband attempts to enter, but is met with a hard push and a locked door. At this, he begs for forgiveness.

"Forgiveness?!" scoffs Margaret. "You're a damn drunkard who violated a virgin! You deserve nothing except than the fieriest pits of hell!"

The commander lingers around the balcony, letting the wind wipe away his remaining inebriety.

Many months pass and I imagine during this period, Judy and William immigrate to England. The Wilsons' marriage slowly recover and their second daughter is born the following November. They name her Susan.

The next Chinese New Year falls later in the calendar than most Chinese New Years. In Tai O, the homes are decorated with bright red *fai chun* outside their doors. Children experiment with firecrackers in open spaces and the crackling reminds everyone of sporadic gunfire. Margaret, with a walking Lucy in hand and the infant Susan on a stroller, takes both of them to the island's busy marketplace. There, Lucy proudly sports her cotton-padded *mian ao*, the one her father bought specifically for the holiday. Several onlookers describe the cute toddler as an apple. The noise does not disturb her younger sister, who's enjoying her first nap of the day. Lucy, too, is unafraid of the firecrackers, singing children songs with her mother. I imagine the occasion full of joy; celebration.

It's short lived.

Just before Margaret are her children arrive home, they turn the corner and Margaret's worst nightmare is standing there — albeit skinnier and paler than she remembered. Filling the air is an unfamiliar screaming; the wailing of another infant.

"It's been awhile, Mrs. Wilson," greets Judy, hushing the baby in her arms.

Momentarily stunned by Judy's improved English, Margaret quickly stammers into small talk with her former maid. She speaks long enough to induce a proper conversation then quickly enters her home, though Lucy inexplicitly grabs Judy's hand and leads her inside. The former maid calmly paces the once-familiar living room, pacifying her baby in the process.

"Do you want to see the baby?" Judy asks the child.

Lucy nods.

The former maid leans lower for her to get a good look. Lucy giggles and holds the baby's hand.

"Do you think you two look alike?" jokes Judy.

"NO!" Lucy laughs.

"And why's that?"

"He's a boy! I'm a girl!"

Lucy's innocuous answer pierces Margaret's heart. *Boy...girl...boy...girl...he...she...he...he...*

"You know," hisses Margaret. "I'm sure you Chinese are accustomed to latching onto other people's husbands as second and third concubines, but we British believe in monogamy. Besides — aren't you in love with your boyfriend? That's what the courts will believe anyway...should you make a move on James."

Not intimidated, Judy stiffens, "Mrs. Wilson, standing before you is not the same peasant girl you knew. I am more knowledgeable now. You cannot scare me. I've merely returned to Tai O to *change* the details of the true father in my son's birth certificate."

"No. No, Judy, you can't do that. It would ruin James. Besides — it would technically make you his wife. And you are not his wife. Nor ever will be."

"I will take this court."

"You'll lose."

"I will present the torn clothes from the night of the incident."

"No judge will see it as sufficient evidence, silly girl."

"I have witnesses! William will fly back here and testify. Plus, all those early letters you'd sent us...telling us everything will be fine, your apologies, your direct mentions of...the incident. I've saved those."

The reveal knocks Margaret like a fallen boxer down the canvas. She drops to the couch and covers her face, letting out a piercing, emotional outpour. Judy, feeling guilty of hurting another woman, softens her stance and comforts her. Lucy also comforts her mother.

"Mrs. Wilson," Judy divulges. "When I was in England, I thought about getting an abortion, but I didn't had the courage. My neighbor, a devout Catholic, talked me out of it. Every night she prayed for me and told me that life comes from God and I have no authority to destroy His creations." She looks admirably at her baby. "Fortunately, I saw the light on time."

The room is silent with only Margaret's sniffling.

"I don't intend to cause trouble," adds Judy. "Or to take your husband away from you." She stares out the window. "Besides, William has said he'd take care of me — and Michael."

"Michael..." she whispers my name.

"But I do not fully accept William."

"And why's that?"

My mother, Judy, pauses. "Well...I didn't come from a loving household. I believe because Michael is not William's child, William will eventually neglect him. When I, swung by Mr. Wilson's office today...he...he was very good to the baby. I can see a true father's love in him."

I imagine Margaret swallowing her pride, preventing another outburst when she heard Judy already visiting the commander.

"So what's your plan, exactly?" she asks instead.

"I just want Michael to have his father's surname. I want him to occasionally see and know Mr. Wilson. I believe that'll be important to his development."

Margaret looks down, contemplating the reasoning.

"I can...understand that," she pats Mother. "But ultimately, the decision will be mine and James."

She takes her first good look on Michael, admiring him. Then, Susan's tantrum fills the home and Mother bids Mrs. Wilson goodbye.

Three days later, my mother Judy returns at the home of the Wilsons and they sit uncomfortably silent in the living room. Lucy's contriving *vroom vroom* sounds are all that can be heard as she plays with a double-decker bus model while sitting on her father's lap.

Finally Mr. Wilson utters, "I still feel so awful."

"You should," quips Margaret. "If killing you could make this go away, I'd have poisoned you a long time ago."

"Please spare the theatrics," interrupts Mother. "All I want is to know what you've decided. Have you both made a decision yet?"

The commander lowers his head, withholding the answer.

Margaret speaks for them, "We're...okay with Michael carrying James' surname. But we have some, shall we say, terms and conditions."

"I did not come for 'conditions'," Mother snaps. "I have come for only a direct 'yes' or 'no' answer. So, I ask again: have you decided on accepting my proposal yet?"

The commander straightens himself, gesturing for his former maid to calm down.

"Yes, okay? A hundred apologies with it. The answer's yes. Michael can take my last name."

"I want to be clear. I just want the surname because Michael can live a dignified life. Nothing more. I do not have any desire to marry such a *damn foreigner* like you."

The term angers Mr. Wilson.

"I'll let that slide this time," he pauses for thought. "But what I suggest is that you change your surname to 'Wilson' as well. Having a British name can give you power, Judy. Especially in this society."

"I will...think about it," mutters my mother. "Perhaps if I see the surname going well for my son growing up."

"And I'll definitely be there for Michael," the commander promises. "I'll take him to parks. Show him around. But...and here are the terms and conditions...I don't want Michael growing up with your father and family. They're a bunch of uncouth sailors, lowlifes that'll negatively influence him."

My mother nods.

"And one more thing," finishes Mr. Wilson. "Because of my promotion, they'll be giving Margaret and I a new apartment. The paperwork is almost done. We can give you this house here. We'll cover the rent, of course, but you have to understand because of its high price, there won't be much left for allowance. You'll have to live frugally."

"I accept," agrees Mother. "I do not need a high allowance, only enough to get by. But you must pay for all of Michael's education."

"Certainly," Mr. Wilson smiles. "Only the best for my Michael. After all, I have plans for him graduating Cambridge or Oxford one day."

Margaret sits, biting her tongue.

Chapter 11

Around this time period, many American war veterans are stationed in Hong Kong to prepare for the Korean War. The China Fleet Club is packed every night, filled with soldiers who want to experience the city they dub 'The Pearl of the Orient'. They drink as if there's no promised tomorrow. Even Commissioner McGrady has lost his usual spot, resorting to sitting alongside the lesser officers at the bar. The bartender, though, has gotten wise to Father, and now he is always given a fizzy drink, prompting a new officer, straight from Scotland Yard, to inquire, "I do say Commander, why don't I ever see you take a *real* drink? Hahaha!"

Antoher officer laughs. "That's 'cause the commander can't handle his liquor, mate!" he teases.

My father gives him a stern glare.

"Aw, don't let 'em get to you, James," calms Commissioner McGrady, "You know, I don't know whether to envy or be jealous of you. Try as I might with the missus, we've yet to have our first child. But you, dear boy — you've managed to squeeze in *three* children in under two years."

"What?" gawks the transplant officer. "Three children in under two years? Mate, you having twins?"

My father merely smiles and shakes his head.

"Aye," adds his drunken colleague. "Look 'ere, mate. I think ya lucky, eh? Me missus— she ain't done me a favor producin' no children. Perhaps I shall find me a new woman who'll substitute, eh?"

"The fault, maybe, lies with you," jibes Father. "Perhaps there's an issue with your inner workings. Don't be so quick to blame the woman."

The Commissioner gets into the middle of the building argument and calms down Father.

"Just ignore them, James," he advises. "They're just drunkards — the lot of 'em." He produces a small envelope from his jacket. "Now this — this is worth your time. Have a look. Tell me what you think."

Father gives him a curious stare; it wasn't like the commissioner to discuss work in leisure hours.

"Relax," his boss smiles. "It's about your new house. We've narrowed it down to two locations. One is above your current home, higher along the mountain and a fabulous view of Tai O. The other is in Mui Wo, an area of Lantau Island northeast of Tai O. You can easily take your wife and daughters to the beaches there."

Father thinks for a moment then asks, "Which one do you suggest, commissioner?"

"Most definitely, Mui Wo. When I first moved here, that's where I lived. It's gorgeous, James. Absolutely gorgeous. I'm certain Margaret will agree with this assessment."

My father responses with a polite nod.

On the ferry ride back, he take out the two house photos and makes a quick decision. He places one of the photos in his pocket while dumping the other in the trash.

Many months later, my mother moves into the my father's former house with little fanfare. She makes dinner for her brother and a few friends as appreciation for their help.

Meanwhile, Mrs. Wilson enjoys the mountaintop view of their new apartment. She can see half the island and its numerous fishing villages, though the walk past their old home taints a bit of her satisfaction.

Initially, she had been opposed.

"My dear," she asked when first hearing of Father's decision. "With your new title, surely you could've moved anywhere in Tai O, let alone Lantau Island. Why stay in the same area?"

"Tai O is vulnerable for contraband and smugglers," he reasons. "This is where I'm needed. Besides...it's where the cannon's located."

Though this was a half-truth.

I know his primary reason is to catch a glimpse of me. When my mother is teaching me how to walk outside or I'm crawling inside the sandlot at the park. He sees me twice a day to and from work, never engaging us, staring, I imagine, only from a distance. I believe Mother intentionally showcasing me during those times because she wants for me to be seen. My father is happy, and quite in love, with me, his only son.

One day, however, he sees my mother attending to me, my tiny arm soaking in blood. Dropping his passive charade, my father walks up to us and immediately carries me to the local clinic. My mother follows, telling him it's a cut. As I'm being ushered into the doctor's office, my father stops Mother and tells her she'd be in the way of the staff. He asks her what happens, but she's too concerned to respond. When the doctor brings me out, I pretend to cry to get the attention of Mother, smiling back only after she carries me onto her shoulder. The three of us share a rare moment of happiness.

"You hungry?" Father asks.

My mother smiles and nods.

We are taken to a local noodle house. The rumors of what happened between my mother and father have, up to this point, been mere gossip on the island. Now, in plain view, we are visual proof of their sin. At the noodle house, Mother is uncomfortable with two patrons openly talking about her. Their chatter is obvious, without attempt of concealment. At first, Father ignores this, ordering fish egg noodles for Mother and a bowl of beef brisket noodles for himself. I get fish congee. When it arrives, Father takes the manager aside and asks him to silent the gossiping patrons.

"But sir," pleads the manager. "To do so would be difficult."

Father changes his mood and threatens, "As the police commander of this island, I can expedite your renewal license pending at my desk. Or, on the other hand, if I were to be inclined, also hinder it to the point where your business would no longer exist."

The manager swallows hard and thinks, then begrudgingly walks over to the patrons.

"Hey!" he screams at them. "If you're going to disturb the customers here, do it under your own time — outside!"

The gossiping patrons grow scared and leave. With just the three of us, we eat alone like royalty. Mother looks admirably at my father, basking in the power she feels around him. He notices and offers to take the burden of feeding me.

"Your fish egg noodles are getting cold," he insists.

Mother smiles and hands my fish congee to him. Bite by bite my father feeds me, occasionally zipping the spoon away from me at the last moment. My infant self laughs. Father adores me, loves my blue eyes...the same blue eyes that are similar to my step-sisters'. He's not too keen on my small nose, however. I know Mother well enough to imagine what she's doing now. She's polite, pretending to not notice and eat, though she can't help but smile at how wonderful Father treats me.

When he escorts her home, Mother thanks him.

"What for?" asks Father.

"For your help today. I wouldn't know what to do with Michael hurt."

He brushes off her compliment, "I'm doing what any father would do."

"Not so. My father would never show any affection towards me. He only knew how to yell at my brothers and tell me I wasn't good."

"Well, it's important how we talk and treat children, Judy. It affects who they'll become some day."

My mother stares at him and, this time, doesn't hide her reverence.

When he returns home, Father finds Mrs. Wilson awake and nervously waiting for him. As Father is not prone to lying, he tells his wife everything that's happened.

The following morning, after Mother has fed me and attended to drying laundry from the balcony's makeshift bamboo rack, she sees a familiar woman walking down the mountain. At first, she pays no mind to it because it's not unusual to spot Mrs. Wilson walking past our house for the marketplace. Mother sifts through the refrigerator to discover a lack of food and immediately heads outside to buy groceries. Surprisingly, she finds Mrs. Wilson waiting at the front door. Mrs. Wilson is alone and angry.

"Where's Michael?" she demands.

Without waiting for a response, Mrs. Wilson brisk past Mother and beelines to my crib in the dining room. She immediately yanks my left arm and forcefully lifts my sleeve. The coercion causes me to wail. Mother immediately comes to my rescue, taking me away from Mrs. Wilson.

"Are you insane?" screams Mother. "He's a mere child!"

Mrs. Wilson feels a tinge of guilt and apologies.

"James told me about last night. All of it. The wound, the hospital...I...I just wanted to see if your son was alright."

"Yeah? I know why you're really here," Mother seethes. "But you need to calm down. This isn't helping anyone."

"Oh, but I *am* helping — helping to see if the mother of a defenseless child is deliberately hurting him. Helping to see if I should alert the authorities."

"What? You're insane! If you think I'd intentionally hurt my own son to get your husband's attention —"

"Yeah, I'm saying that," she glares at my mother. "You know, since I heard what happened, I've suspected your son's injury was deliberate."

Mother walks nose to nose with Mrs. Wilson.

"Oh yeah? Prove it," she challenged.

Margaret leads Mother to the kitchen, specifically pointing to a corner and ridicules, "I've lived here three years and know every nook and cranny of this house, particularly this kitchen. This corner right here? It's horribly designed, narrow but the only area to set a decent cutting board. Lucy used to grab me with her dominant hand while I was cutting — I can't tell you how many times I almost injured her. I presume your son does the same thing. But look at which hand he's holding his bottle at the moment; his right — his dominant hand. If you really cut him by accident, and let's face it, this is the only area to use knives, then why is his *left arm* hurt instead?"

My mother looks at Mrs. Wilson like the Englishwoman's an idiot.

"He is *using* his right hand because his left hand is *injured*," she states matter-of-factly. Mother then takes out a knife. "Look at this tip. It's bent. It's bent because I dropped it."

"You could've staged it that way," accuses Mrs. Wilson.

She backs off and heads towards the door.

"I'll be keeping an eye on you, Judy" she warns.

"Oh yeah?" Mother barks behind. "Remember it's your husband's duty to be a responsible father to Michael! Even you can't stop that!"

The door slams with such ferocity that that my toddler self cries. Mother hushes me in her arms.

"I'm so sorry, Michael. I won't let that mean woman hurt you. Mama will protect you."

True to his word, Father continues to be a good dad and visits me every day after work. He loves it when he kisses me and I giggle at his prickly beard. Eventually, he sees me even during his days off, especially at the holidays. Mother is always with us, which infuriates Mrs. Wilson.

One day, he returns home from spending time with me at the park and finds Lucy and Susan fighting over a cookie jar.

"Daddy," asks Lucy. "Help us open this cookie jar."

"You shouldn't have snacks before dinner," he mutters.

"But we're hungry..."

"Well, dinner's coming up."

"But Mom didn't cook."

Curious, Father immediately goes to the kitchen. It's empty. He goes back to his daughters.

"Lucy, where's Mommy?"

Her tiny finger points to the bedroom. There, he barely sees Margaret under dim lights. She's lying in bed, head to the side of her pillow.

"Dear, what's wrong?" Father rushes to her. Silence.

He searches her head for a fever, finding only a face full of tears.

"What's wrong?" he repeats.

"I don't understand these Chinese women," she mutters. "How they can share with no conscious the husbands of other women." She turns and looks at him. "I certainly couldn't do that."

Father is lost for words.

She adds, "I think it's time for a divorce, James."

The word shatters Father's heart.

"No," he softly speaks. "No...it...it can't be. You are the wife of James Wilson. You are my treasure, my everything. 'Divorce' is the word of the devil. I won't let our marriage falter."

"I saw that woman's cunningness first hand, James. She's full of tricks...lies! That Judy witch will eventually lead to our downfall."

"I swear, Margaret. I'm only doing it for Michael. I could care less about that dark-skinned, filthy peasant."

Mrs. Wilson turns off her tears like a faucet.

"Let's adopt Michael, then. Think about it. He can come over here every day and play with Lucy and Susan. They'd love little Michael."

"That's...that's a good idea, darling. But you wouldn't mind the extra work?"

"Oh no, James...no. For unity, I'd go the extra mile."

Father kisses her.

"Alright, that settles it. We're adopting him." He nods toward the living room. "Come on, our daughters need their mommy."

"I'm sorry. I forgot to cook. Can you please help me prepare?"

As Lucy and Susan sees their parents head to the kitchen, Susan crawls over and Father has to carry her away from her mother. He apologies to his wife and keeps the girls occupied, playing dolls with them.

When Mother heard of Father's suggestion to adopt me, she is displeased, but knew there is little choice. The first day of my adoption, Mother dresses me in a Donald Duck shirt, long stockings and a pair of black shoes. I know I look adorable. Father is very happy when he sees me.

"Mommy," I reach out to Mother.

Father kisses my face, "Mommy can't come along, but you'll have your sisters to play with."

I make a face.

"What?" asks Father.

"Girls...yucky," I blurt.

"Why are they yucky? Girls aren't yucky."

Mother explains that in the park, I would push girls down the slide.

"You can't do that, Michael," Father shakes his head.

"I spank him when he does that," informs Mother.

"Son," he looks into my eyes. "You have to protect girls, okay? Not hurt them. Because that's what boys do. We look out for the girls."

He takes me out and enjoys his time with me as we walk up the mountaintop. My father feels a higher love for me over his daughters. When we near his home, Father looks at me and instructs, "Now, Michael, listen carefully. There's going to be a woman in there and you will call her Mrs. Wilson."

"Mrs. Wilson," I repeat.

"Good...good boy."

"The two little girls are Lucy and Susan. Can you repeat their names back to me?"

"Lucy...Susan..."

"Excellent. What a smart boy you are!"

Father takes me inside. The home is large and spacious, nothing I'm used to in Tai O. I see the look of several pale skinned people, including a woman approaching to take my jacket.

"Mrs. Wilson," I point at her.

"No," laughs Father. "That's the maid. Let me take you to meet Mrs. Wilson."

He drops me down and takes my hand to the living room. There, I see the real Mrs. Wilson along with two little girls. They're all looking at me with hostility.

"Michael," Father smiles. "How did I teach you to greet her?"

"Mrs. Wilson."

The woman looks at me in a cold tone, not responding to my innocent salutation.

"We'll stick with that," she eventually answers. "Just don't ever call me 'Mother'."

When the day is over and I am taken back home to my real mother, she gives me a shower and I imagine this is what takes place:

Mother asks, "Did you had fun at Daddy's house today?"

I frown and Mother repeats the question, scrubbing me.

"No," I mutter, looking away.

"I thought you'd have fun there. There are so many toys."

"All girl toys."

"Still toys, Michael."

I continue avoiding eye contact with Mother.

"They yell at me."

"Who?"

I didn't know how to answer or couldn't.

"Was it the girls? Did they yell at you, Michael?"

I nod.

"Very mean," I look at Mother.

She pauses, then asks, "What about Mrs. Wilson? Was she mean too?"

I hesitate then slowly respond, "She yell at me because I touch her piano."

When Father comes the next day, Mother hesitates to open the door. After much persistency, she lets in my Father, telling him I'm sick. He approaches my crib where I'm coughing, but I'm happy to see him. He immediately lifts me and kisses me.

"I don't understand," Father says to Mother. "He seemed okay yesterday."

"He was crying in the middle of the night. When I checked him, he was hot as a stove."

Father glances at Mother.

"And you didn't tell me this, Judy? You know I would've rushed him to the hospital."

Mother hesitates then blurts out, "And your wife...she would've been okay with you coming here to do that?"

Father bites his lip, knowing her meaning.

Chapter 12

Since then, I've stopped coming to Father's house. Instead, he visits me at our home, much like before the adoption. Mother would make soup for him, but after Father finishes it, she hastens him to leave.

"Please," pleads Father. "I just want to spend a little more time with Michael."

"Your wife wouldn't like that," she reminds.

Whenever he leaves, he asks a kiss from me, then attempts one from Mother. It takes many visits before Mother accepts. Now, all she does is kiss him.

One surprising Sunday afternoon, the day he least visits, she's surprise to find him standing in our front door. Mother asks, "Don't you go to church on Sundays?"

"Margaret's gone," he dismisses. "She's not in town anymore. Her mother's very sick in England, so she took the kids with her."

Following this, he begins to spend the night with us. I love sleeping between him and Mother, feeling a nest of safety and assurance. But always, I would find myself waking up in my crib the next morning.

In time, even though I stop visiting Father's home, he does occasionally take me to the police station and from there, I play with my two step-sisters.

As the years pass, I grow up with Lucy and Susan, attending the same schools and making the same friends.

On Susan's sixth birthday, Mother and I are officially invited to their mountaintop home. Mother gives Mrs. Wilson her daughter's present and then offers to help in the kitchen. Being the only boy there, I grow tired of the girls and explore the house. I find Father sitting alone in one of the rooms, practicing a guitar.

"Daddy, can you teach me how to play your piano?" I point at his guitar.

"This isn't a piano, dear Michael. It's called a guitar. Come, let me show you how to play..."

I jump on his lap and hold it, enjoying the random noise that comes from the strumming. Father guides my tiny hands and fools me into thinking I'm making beautiful music on my own. I giggle and he laughs; we're having a jolly good time —

— until an intense yelling comes from the kitchen and Father shoots up and takes me with him. We immediately arrive on the spot where a crowd gathers between Mother and Mrs. Wilson in a heated argument. I have never heard Mother utter such dirty language and her emotions dismantle her usual fluent English.

"I...am...not...a witch!!!" screams Mother. "Do not call me that! I am *not* the fucking devil! You call me devil! I am not a fucking devil!"

"This woman," Mrs. Wilson announces. "Once intentionally cut her son's arm to get the attention of my husband. Can you believe that? She seduces my husband and sleeps with him! You should be totally ashamed of yourself, you whorish hell spawn! Get out! You don't belong here!"

"I...here...because...of..." Mother clutches her heart, catching her breath. "I'm...here...for...you...out of...respect!"

"Silly chinawoman."

"You...invite me...to...ridicule...me..."

"What's wrong with your English, mmm? Suddenly your fluency falls apart like your charade to being civilized!"

"Fuck to shit...*damn foreigner*!!"

The term triggers Mrs. Wilson into a new level of rage. To the crowd's amusement, she rushes at Mother to hit her, but Father catches her arm in time and restrains her.

"Go, Judy," he orders.

I am taken by hand as we exit their home. Mother leaves in a string of cursing.

When we arrive home that same afternoon, Mother changes me and then looks seriously into my eyes.

"Son," she orders. "Listen very, very carefully. You will study hard, you will do well in school, you will succeed and you will achieve more than anything that *damn foreigner* and her *damn daughters* will ever achieve." She pulls me closer. "You represent me, do you understand? You represent *us*. We are *not* a mistake. We are *not* an accident. Understand?"

I nod.

She kisses my forehead.

"Good boy."

Since then, Mother vows to never speak with Mrs. Wilson again. Years pass and I fulfill my promise, averaging higher test scores that the Wilson daughters, though I struggle with English. Lucy and Susan have an advantage there, being raised in a British household.

By the time I'm ten-years-old, Mother pushes Father to tutor me, though his wife impedes this, causing friction in the Wilsons' relationship.

"Father," I ask him one day. "Besides English, can you teach me how to play the guitar?"

"Of course," smiles Father. "I've always wanted to teach you."

Mother hears this and, with a heavy heart, expresses her discontent.

"Michael, I don't mind you having hobbies, but don't

let it take priority over studying. School must always come first," she warns.

"This isn't a *hobby*," I challenge. "I'm going to take guitar playing seriously."

Father intervenes and cheerily remarks, "Now Judy, Michael's a bright young man. I'm sure he can be serious for both his schoolwork and his passions, won't you son? If you want to learn guitar so bad, I'll get you one."

True to his word, I receive a brand new acoustic guitar the next day. I cherish and treat it like my most prized possession, practicing every night. Unfortunately, I also prove Father wrong. My grades drastically falter and on my next progress report, they are much lower than Susan's — Mother is beyond furious. I give my best excuses, but Mother will have none of it. Eventually, I feel so ashamed that I walk around like a convict. My head is down and I don't dare make eye contact with Mother.

Then, one day, she surprisingly plops something next to me and I examine her new gift.

"I got it from the stationary store," she explains. "I believe writing a diary will improve your writing skills."

I look at it with disinterest, then look up at Mother.

"Not only will it improve your writing skills," she adds. "I hope that by writing on it, you'll read your entries when you're older and realize what an immature, disobedient dolt you were."

I apologetically rise from my chair.

"I love you," I whisper, a few tears falling from my eyes.

After a few weeks, Mother comes back to me and criticizes, "Michael, you're not writing useful topics in your diary. It's all about sports, music and your favorite television shows. You need to write about mature things — like school and your plans for the future."

I complain, "But Mother, I've never written on a diary before. I just know that I'm supposed to express my thoughts and hobbies. Isn't that the point of keeping a journal? And besides, if you're going to snoop into my entries, I'll be keeping them secret from you."

Mother understands, to my surprise.

"Okay," she nods. "I won't read it anymore then. But promise me, Michael, write more meaningful topics and plan your life accordingly."

"Yes, mum."

"Good," she kisses my forehead. "I love you."

I since have written deeper, more thoughtful topics as per Mother's request. However, I decide to lock it in a box and store in a closet, just in case.

It's present day again.

I've spent a week fusing Father's diaries and mine together; I piece our whole history. Since this time, I've only left my hotel room during housekeeping interruptions and the occasional restaurant visit. The day's weather, however, is clear blue skies and gorgeous weather. It's a good excuse to venture around Tai O, exploring the old haunts with Father's diary fresh in my mind. As I explore, the scenes appear vivid to me; I blend together past and present. The makeshift sheet metal home where my mother was raised is now even more derelict and rusting. She used to take me back here to visit Grandfather and the open area beside it is where my uncle and I played football, currently occupied by two girls jumping rope. I then make my way to the mooring post, the scene of my first fishing lesson with my uncle. It feels like only yesterday that I screamed so loudly after catching my first fish that Mother and Grandfather thought I'd fell into the ocean. They came rushing out of Grandfather's home only to breathe a sigh of relief. I remember jumping up and down, proudly presenting my first red snapper.

Getting back to the present, I start returning to shore but I see an old man and a younger one, leaving Grandfather's former home. I presume they're the current owners. One of the little girls stop jump roping and runs up to them.

"That's the guy!" she points at me.

I walk closer and they look at me, unsure of whether or not to speak English. I ease them with my Cantonese.

"I do apologize for startling you," I say. "I was just caught up in the scenery."

"Ah," nods the younger gentleman. "You must be taking photos then. Happens all the time."

They leave me alone for a few moments, but then I muster up the courage to ask, "Actually, I'm here to find someone local. Perhaps you've heard of him."

The younger gentleman turns towards me and smiles, "Well, you've come to the right person, then." He points at the older gentleman, "My father has lived in Tai O all his life."

"Who're you looking for?" smiles the old man. His teeth are yellow and rotting.

"I'm looking for a former English teacher, very old, if he's still alive."

"Ah, Ol' William Chen," exclaims the old man. "It can only be him. He lives near the hill."

"Yes. He must be pushing eighty," I include.

"Ninety actually," he corrects. "And he's not really an English teacher. Haha. He used to just help the locals translate letters from the former British government. He also taught the local children art."

"Can you tell me where he lives?"

The little girl, shy and hiding behind her father's legs, points at a distance.

"He lives in the white-colored house. Up that hill," she informs.

I wave and thank them.

"I appreciate your help Mr. —?"

"My surname is Gang," he smiles.

"Gang..." The name is familiar to me.

"Yes?" Gang knits his eyebrows. "You've heard of me?"

"Um," I stammer. "W-Well, someone from the area merely mentioned your name because they'd say you might know the whereabouts of William. That's all."

"Ah," he nods. "Well, good luck finding him."

I thank the Gangs again and head for the white-colored house.

As I journey to find William, I pass by my childhood home. I stop at where my Father probably used to stand and I imagine my toddler self, playing with my mother in front. She pretends not to notice the present me, but I know she's aware, even in my imagination. The deserted neighborhood is suddenly transformed to its former glory and the abandoned wasteland before me briefly replenishes its once beautiful greenery. I see playground equipment and children. I'm one of them, shoving girls down the slide. With continued rose-tinted outlook, I walk up the mountain and see an old couple, both wearing cowboy hats, waving at me from their porch. The man nods and takes a sip of his whiskey.

Finally, I arrive at the so-called white-colored home, a one-story stony hut-like building with a sign posted over its front door. In traditional Chinese it reads, 'Silver Forest Studio'. I get back to reality and ring its doorbell. After several attempts, I resort to loudly knocking.

"Excuse me," asks a passing woman with groceries. "Are you looking for Mr. Chen?"

I nod.

"I hear he's in the hospital," she continues. "Something to do with his heart. Which hospital, I'm not too sure."

My heart sinks.

"Is there family around then?" I ask.

She shakes her head. "I'm sorry, Mr. Chen doesn't have family. He lives alone."

Heartbroken, I give up finding William.

The summer sun stubbornly remains in the early evening and I have nothing to do but seek dinner on the island. The area with the greatest amount of restaurants is near the tourist bus stations. I stand amid crowds, trying to decide on which one.

"Sir," cries a voice. "Why don't you try our restaurant? The food here's absolutely amazing!"

She is among dozens of staff members that each restaurant hires to lure customers. This is common with the area and the only way to know which restaurants are actually best is to look for the longest lines. This is how I ended up with the one I'm in now.

"Table for one?" a waiter eventually asks.

I nod and he takes me to a table close to the kitchen. Three young men join and I'm forced to remove my backpack from one of the chairs to accommodate them. In Hong Kong, everyone shares tables.

"What do you recommend?" I ask the waiter.

"Definitely the fried squid cake," he says, immediately finding it on the menu. "It goes excellent with beer. Highly recommended."

"I'll take the squid cake. Add some kind of fish with it. What's a good choice for fish?"

"Oh, you're in for a bit of luck, sir. We've just received a fresh haul of groupers — I saw them myself. Nice quality in all shapes and sizes — and if I may even add a further suggestion, sir, include a vegetable dish mixed with shrimp paste. It'll definitely give you that Tai O flavor!"

"Okay, okay," I laugh. "You've sold me on it. Let's add a small grouper and that vegetable dish you mentioned."

As he leaves, I look at the waiter with admiration. He would've been a fine addition to my restaurant back in Britain.

When I had it, all the available Chinese waiters were recent immigrants from the New Territories — fresh off the countryside and slow as an ox. The people from the inner cities, they're faster on their feet; certainly hungrier and smarter.

When the dishes for the three young men and myself arrive, I pity that they share two of the cheapest dishes on the menu. Seeing how I personally ordered three dishes alone, I invite them to take some of my dinner. At first, they hesitate, but with some small talk, I'm able to make them comfortable to take my food and open up about themselves.

"So you're students," I surmise. "It's good to hear you've chosen America to go to school. The tuition in most of their universities are cheaper than other Western countries, particularly England."

I sit properly and face one of the shy young men.

"Young man," I nod. "Which state have you chosen?"

He timidly answers, " Texas, sir."

"Ah, I see. Although I've only lived in England, I've had many friends from America. So, as you can see, I know a bit about the United States."

His fat friend responds, "The University of Michigan accepted him too, but he chose The University of Houston."

"I see, I see," I nod. "The reputation of The University of Houston is not as good as The University of Michigan."

The fat friend retorts, "But it's warmer in Texas. Plus there's a Chinatown. My friend isn't rich."

"I see, I see."

This is attune to England where the weekends are filled with students who are part-time waiters.

Suddenly, my cell rings.

"Darling," my wife says. "Are you still stuck in that hotel?"

"I'm not there at the moment."

Then, the younger, sweeter voice of my daughter chimes, "I'm here too, Daddy! I've brought the baby to see Mum. Did you watch the news on the telly?"

"No," I select my words carefully. "I've...I've been out most of the day. Doing research."

"Well the strike at the airport ends in two days," my wife takes back the phone.

"That's wonderful news. I'll book a flight back immediately."

"Speaking of book, Michael. Have you finished combining the diaries?"

"Almost."

"I won't bother you then. I can't wait to read it, you know. There's so much I'm curious about your childhood."

There's a silence between us. I regret a little about mentioning the diary; there're some things about my past I'd rather she didn't know. My wife and I exchange a pleasant farewell. The three students I share the table with are now gone. I pay my bill and head back to the Tai O Heritage Hotel. Being the weekend, the nightlife is busy on the island. All around, I hear dogs barking.

Chapter 13

Back at the hotel, I pace back and forth wondering how I should finish the combined diary. My writer's block makes me sleepy and I throw myself to the bed, quickly falling asleep.

Before I know it, I wake to the smooth strumming of Father's guitar. I see him, calmly sitting on the leather seat next to the lamp. A pair of familiar hands stroke my face and I turn and see Mother, resting my head on her lap. This is how I wanted us — together and full of unity. The tranquil scene doesn't last long, however, as I notice Father's strumming getting off-tune and grating. The sound becomes unbearable and Mother angrily walks over and whisks his guitar away. I blink and the guitar becomes a feather duster in her hands. She hits me and hits me, telling me to study harder and be more successful than the Wilson daughters. I dodge and cover myself from her attacks, screaming for mercy. Mother finally shoves me and I find myself hitting the ground, opening my eyes back to reality.

It is three o'clock in the morning.

I rise and head for my laptop. I suddenly know how to finish the combined diary.

Now that I'm in my later teenage years, Mother pushes me to become a doctor. But because I'm scared of blood, she brings home a live chicken from the market, hoping to instill some courage. She doesn't say a word as she leads me to the kitchen.

"Hold this," she hands me a knife. Then, handing me the flapping chicken, orders, "Now hold this chicken."

I hesitate, holding the knife and watching the chicken flap around in her grip.

"Like this," she orders, forcing its wings together then handing it to me. "This way, it won't fly away."

But my nervousness makes me drop the chicken and we watch it scrawling around the kitchen. Mother tsks and calmly grabs it back, then repeats her handoff.

"Don't be afraid now," she explains. "I'm just teaching you how to kill a chicken."

She takes my shaking hand and makes me pinpoint the area where I can separate the chicken's trachea and esophagus.

"Now watch very carefully, Michael."

In a split-second, she lifts the chicken's head up, holding my hand with her other one to make sure the chicken's secure.

"You got to get it right in the trachea. If you do it wrong, it won't die right away."

My other hand shakes vibrantly, almost dropping the knife. Mother forces it still and, in one swift motion, puppeteers it to savagely slash the chicken's throat. The violent action forces the blood to gush all over my hands. It's warm and thick. Somewhere I hear the clanging of my dropped knife. My eyes are wide open as they focus on the red dripping from my hand and the flapping of the chicken, still alive, shocks me to toss it to the tile floor. The kitchen is now filled with blood as the chicken runs everywhere. then collpases. I watch the chicken's eyes, half-opened and dragging its legs to get away, slowly dying a painful, suffering death.

"Help me boil some water," Mother instructs. "I need it to pluck its feathers."

But I ignore her orders and ran to the bathroom to lock myself. I continue to shake as I peer in the sink mirror. I look like one of the murderers in the telly shows. Immediately, I strip naked and rush to the sink, repeatedly scrubbing myself with a bar of soap. After thirty minutes, I finally muster the courage to slip out of the bathroom. Dinner is already set and Mother is calmly sitting at the dining table. Even the blood is all gone from the kitchen.

"Come on, son. Dinner's ready."

I nervously sit and, although I'm not religious, I clumsily re-enact the ways I saw the Catholics say grace. When my eyes open from the prayer, I notice the chicken nicely fresh and cooked in the middle of the other dishes.

"Well. Don't just look at it," insists Mother.

She takes her chopsticks and puts a chicken leg in my bowl. Half-an-hour ago, I was watching that same leg twitch and walk; now it's on top of my rice. I passively skirt it away from the other food, eating just enough to get full. I then excuse myself and hide in my room.

The following week, Mother continues to bring home live chickens and the hideous act repeats. I reiterate the same fear but slowly, it becomes replaced with detachment. I realize that blood is part of nature and if I'm going to be a doctor, I'll need to get used to it. However, the detachment has also made me prone to temperament. My mood of late has been unstable and one night, as Mother is nagging, I suddenly throw my bowl on the ground and head to my room. It isn't until the next day that I learn one of the broken pieces cut my Mother's toe and I feel immense guilt.

She doesn't talk to me for a week.

Whenever I'm depressed now, I seek out Father. He's usually at the China Fleet Club. Father is understanding, much more calm than Mother. Over time, I grow use to the presence of foreigners — even if they're not all Englishmen, they speak English. My favorite moments are when Father performs with a band in the stage area. Lucy and Susan are also there watching him. I like walking on stage when no one's performing, observing the drums and bass guitars. Even if they're inanimate steel, the instruments pulse with life.

Like a child in a toy store, I approach the drum set and randomly hit and bang, creating noise that has no form, no grace. Father laughs and takes me aside, showing me how it's properly done. He sticks to a catchy rhythm, getting a cohesive and gratifying sound from the right drum combinations. Each drum serves its collectivist function, part of a wonderful fabric of music that draws a large applause from the China Fleet Club when Father is done. Among the loudest cheers come from my step-sisters as Lucy runs up stage to kiss her Father.

Susan joins and Father turns and gathers us for a huddle.

"I've got an idea," he smiles. "Since you've all got the Wilson music gene in you, why don't we do a song together as a family. You know, like the Jackson 5."

He holds his grin, expecting us to get excited but we only return baffled looks.

"Can I be the lead singer?" Lucy insists.

"Oh, of course," laughs Father. "You have the sweetest voice, Lucy. Susan, why don't you do backup and Michael, you play the guitar."

"But who'll do the drums?" asks Susan.

Father scoffs, "Me, of course. The drummer is like a captain of the ship. With me at the helm, I'll steer us — alright, let's give this crowd something to remember. Let's play The Supremes' 'Where Did Our Love Go?'"

Lucy and Susan walks to the mics to get ready, but Father sees me hesitating.

"I...I don't think I can do it," I look at him.

He takes me backstage and slides the most magnificent thing I've seen — an electric guitar.

"Wow!" I blurt out.

Father shows me how to operate it, telling the functions of the various buttons. His confidence in me gives me courage and I walk back on stage with handwritten music notes. Within minutes, the four of us are jamming, pleasing the stage with our cover of The Supremes.

"WhoooooOOOO!" I yell as we finish. "Did you guys see me? I...I'm a musical genius! It was my first time with an electrical guitar and I was perfect!"

But Father takes me down a notch.

"You were out of rhythm the whole time," he says. "And a lot of those notes were incorrect."

Lucy joins the criticism, "Yeah, Michael, you were only focused on yourself, playing in your own little world!"

I suddenly bow my head in shame, "I'm sorry."

Their words pops my balloon of self-assurance.

Seeing me humbled, Father rests a hand on my shoulder.

"Hey, this is normal. It's our first performance together, Michael. I thought we did pretty good for our first try," he cheers.

We pack up the instruments and return the stage to pristine condition.

"Alright, kids," Father gives us a farewell. "I'll be going now. But hey — I'll set up a sound booth for you at Queen's Building at Central every Sunday. It's owned by the

Gold Records Company. I can hook you up with the executives there."

The three of us are elated.

Our band forms within two weeks, but with Father out as drummer, we need a replacement. Fortunately, Lucy has her boyfriend Dennis, a half-Chinese, half-Portuguese talent, whose tall and thin frame sometimes makes him stoop to play. He isn't too bad and even introduces a friend to play bass guitar. Later, with the help of the Filipino professionals, we vastly improve, ready for competition.

My grades freefall.

The latest progress report shows me diving under the top ten students of my class and Mother becomes furious.

"If you don't rise back to the top ten in your next report card," she threatens. "I'm taking your guitar and band privileges away."

I don't respond.

"Do you understand, Michael?" she presses.

"I *understand*," I sarcastically reply.

"You understand, do you? What exactly do you understand? Tell me, do you understand enough to stop spending time with those *damn foreigner* step-sisters? Do you understand how humiliating we'd look if you screw up and they achieve greater success than you?"

"Alright, alright!" I angrily wave off. "I get it, okay?! You don't have to nag me all the time!"

A year later, the Wilsons move out of Tai O and closer to the inner city, but my step-sisters still attend the same school as me. One day, after class, Lucy and Susan break away from their usual circle of friends to discuss *Lusan and the Thunder* with me.

"Don't forget we're performing at the YMCA this Saturday," Lucy reminds.

I shyly shake my head.

"I-I'm sorry, Lucy, but I can't make it. I have to study."

My step-sister is not the type who takes rejection well. She sneers and I feel intimidated. Fortunately, Susan's interjects.

"Isn't the performance the following Saturday?" she corrects Lucy.

I breathe a sigh of relief.

"Oh," I smile. "In that case, then, it's no big deal. I can make it."

Lucy slightly softens her demeanor.

Due to last year's poor grades, I study harder for my finals. Mother sees me buried in books, sometimes on near-sleepless nights. Consequently, I go to each of the tests with full confidence, knowing I'd do well in them before the results arrive. As my reward, I'm able to go perform at the YMCA without having to sneak off like usual.

We play well that night, but the adrenaline of performing in front of a supportive crowd quickly dissipates. Drowsiness takes over and suddenly I'm feeling like sea fog. Filipino Tony notices this and, after a song, pulls me aside and commands me to go to a toilet stall with him.

"Lock the door, Michael."

I do as he says. He takes out a tiny bag of white powder and carefully pours the contents onto a small piece of aluminum foil. I watch him toss away the empty bag and bring out a lighter to heat the foil from under. Gradually, a visible stream of smoke arise.

"Breathe it," he orders.

I hesitate for a moment, then plant my face above it. My nose feels a shocking sting and I fall back hard, banging my head on the stall. Whether it's from the hit or the substance itself, I feel an immense rush of energy. Tony laughs and snorts the rest for himself. He struts out of the bathroom and from a distance I hear Susan's voice.

"Michael, where are you? Can you come back on stage, please?"

I get back and perform.

It isn't until well over midnight I return home.

Whenever I'm feeling down, the first person I seek is Tony. I constantly find him at practice and ask for his powder. I love how I feel afterwards. One day, my awareness is so numb that I didn't even comprehend Uncle Lou dragging me to his office.

"God damn it," he mutters. "You're high, aren't you?"

"W-what?"

"Are you taking drugs, Michael?"

I blink for a moment then realize the shame.

"That idiot Tony!" Uncle Lou curses. "I told your father it'd be a bad idea to connect you guys. Your father said it was okay, that you were so clean-cut that you'd be incorruptible. But here we are — you standing here, high in my office!"

I started crying.

"P-please don't tell Father, Uncle Lou."

He stares for a moment, then sighs.

"Touch that stuff again and I won't be so tight-lipped. Dismissed."

I leave the room with puffy eyes. Susan passes and immediately confronts me.

"Michael, what's wrong? Why're your eyes puffy? What were you doing inside Uncle Lou's office?"

"Ah, it's nothing," I lie. "Lack of sleep, I guess. Uncle Lou and I were just discussing...um...performance schedules."

But my cold-turkey withdrawal has resulted in moodiness and ill-temperament. I constantly find myself drinking water. Fortunately, there isn't school responsibilities during my recovery period. Two weeks later, I'm my normal self again, but I avoid speaking to Tony at practice.

Everything is dull and predictable when the next semester arrives. My step-sisters and I go to school and perform like usual. The only peculiarity is Father's constant absence; no one's heard from him, including Lucy and Susan. When I finally muster the courage to ask, Susan responds, "There's supposedly an internal investigation on massive police corruption."

"Really? Do you think they're suspecting Father?" I ask.

"Well," shrugs Susan. "I don't think he's corrupted. Most corrupt coppers live in luxury. That's the telling sign. We've been living modestly. It would be a great surprise to find him corrupted."

I look forward in silence.

An unfortunate wave of school tests and band

performances come my way and I fold under pressure. My abstinence from drugs ends when I call Tony, begging for a hit.

"Go to Irene," he says. "She has some samples at her home."

I immediately rush to Irene's apartment, ringing the doorbell several times before the sultry Filipina opens the door. I find her blurry-eyed and groggy. She's wearing a long t-shirt that covers down to her thighs.

"Tony sent me," I inform.

She lets me in and I storm through her living room, looking in all directions for heroin.

"They're in there," she points at her bedroom.

I stumble into it and hear her turn on the shower. She hums inside the bathroom while I flip through cabinets and boxes, finally finding the herion I sought. I quickly find some foil, but there's no lighter. Irene stops humming and I hear the shower curtain fold back. She comes out soaking wet in a bathrobe.

"You looking for this?" she tosses a lighter.

I catch it and immediately set the powder to the foil. When the familiar smoke arises, I greedily sniff it and Irene comes over and inhales the rest. We sit on the floor for a moment, high and intense. She bends down a little and I make no secret about staring at her breasts. I start to shake when she smiles and removes her bathrobe entirely. I'm stunned by her dark-skinned beauty, but she is comfortable with the moment. The next thing I know, her arms are around me and my blood rises.

It is my first time and I finish quickly. I breathe heavily and apologize.

"I'm sorry, Irene...I..."

"It's your first time, wasn't it?"

I nod and brace myself for her taunts, but she praises me instead.

"That was pretty good for your first time, Michael."

She kisses my forehead.

I casually get dress, but she stops me.

"Forgetting my money?" she hints.

I shake and damn myself — I should've known better than to think there are free things in this world. Since I don't know how much I owed, I unload all my bills.

"Is that enough?" I blurt.

Irene laughs as she rolls up the money and slips it between her breasts.

"I'm not a prostitute," she kisses me. "But the drugs aren't free."

I leave her apartment feeling like a man. It's exciting not feeling guilty anymore, unashamed of being wild and tap dancing to life's recklessness. Over time, I begin to hang out with Irene. We repeat our drug and sexual escapades. I know she doesn't love me, but whatever brief depression I have quickly fades whenever I see that dark beautiful body.

My problems are eventually numbed.

Chapter 14

What happens next, I'm uncertain to put into context or meaning. All I know is that the moment forces our actions. Perhaps, as the Buddhists say, moments happen as opportunities for self-interpretation. But perhaps, as the Christians say, moments happen because they're tests — and under this philosophy, I've failed. I don't know exactly what forces create the moment, only that what happens next is something that shouldn't have happened.

But it did.

Perhaps all tragedies are created this way.

It's the first of July, the Hong Kong Observatory issues a typhoon warning and all my classes are cancelled. Mother wants me to spend this time studying, but all I can think about are doing drugs. I'm easily agitated and sweat a lot. I distract myself with guitar playing, reminiscing on the smoky white powder. Mother doesn't like my guitar blaring and lectures me from my locked door. I drown her nagging out with louder playing and her nagging graduates into an intense door kicking. Then, it abruptly stops. Curious, I halt myself and listen.

Amid the ambient raining, I make out Father's voice.

It's strange that he's here during the severe weather. Carefully, I slightly open my door to eavesdrop on my parents' conversation. They're in the dining room. Father is holding a beer bottle and looks intoxicated.

"Have you been drinking again?" yells Mother.

"Relax," Father dismisses. "It's just a beer."

"Look at you...you're drunk! You've had quite a few already, I know it!"

Father rolls his eyes and takes a long sip of his bottle. After a moment he says, "Commissioner McGrady is retiring next year and he's put me up as his top replacement."

Mother's expression graduates to optimism — but Father's solemnness betrays that anticipation. He takes her hand and tells her to sit down. He spies me peeking from the corner and invites me to join them. I slowly open the door and obey.

"You've heard about the massive corruption going with the Hong Kong Police Force?" Father asks.

We both nod.

"Are you part of the corruption?" inquires Mother.

"No...if I was, the Commissioner wouldn't have considered me for promotion."

"So what's happening?" asks Mother.

"The commissioner, well, he wants me to rat out all the corrupt coppers. Problem is, a vast majority of my men are corrupted too. I'll be burning a lot of bridges."

"Then just give him a short list. Just give him the officers you don't like."

Father laughs and I can smell the alcohol from his breath.

"You really don't get it do you, Judy? The commissioner probably has a complete list of corrupted officers. He's doing this to test me; to see if I can turn against my own men. Do you know what all these men would do if I rat them out? This isn't like what happened with Wah Chai.

This is a majority of the police force we're talking about!"

"Then decline the promotion," Mother advises.

Father sighs and leans back on our sofa. He stares into the ceiling and I start returning to my room.

"Michael," he stops me. His hand reaches to his coat pocket and exposes the music contest application. My eyes grow wide, but Mother whisks it away. She quickly reads the label and shakes her head.

"No!" she declares. "He's already spent too much with his music."

"Aw, come on Judy. It's from Uncle Lou at the Gold Records Company. Let the young man have some fun. He needs to socialize at his age — have some hobbies."

Father turns and smiles at me, but frowns when he notices my constant shaking and sweating. I involuntarily sniff.

"Do you have a cold, Michael?" Mother asks. "You're shaking and sniffling."

"Y-yes," I lie. "I just got sick recently. Must be the weather change."

Father may be half-drunk, but wise to my dishonesty. He pulls out a bag of the familiar white powder. My eyes widen in shock. The corner of my mouth betrays me and slightly salivates. Father puts it back in his pocket.

"Got that from a recent bust today," Father says sternly. "You seem to be highly familiar with it."

I stand shocked as we stare, reading each other's minds. My eyes tell the truth. This must be the main reason for his visit...the promotion debate, the music application...all of it was a cover up to test my heroin usage.

"So the rumors are true," Father mutters.

"What's happening?" Mother asks. "Michael, what's going on?"

I blink and lose the staring contest, running to my room.

———————

Within minutes, perhaps because of Father's shaming, I feel an intense coldness. I huddle in bed, covering myself with blankets. Mother's banging can be heard.

"What's happening, Michael?" she yells behind the locked door. "This is serious. What're you hiding? Open the door now!"

I curl up in a fetal position. The blankets warm me and I don't feel so cold anymore. Mother's lecturing is now aimed at my father and I get angry and pop out of bed. A wild woman with a deranged look meets me when I open the door. This crazy version of Mother flings me into the living room and demands, "When did you started using drugs, Michael?! Did you do them in this house?! TELL ME!"

"Mother!" I cry, fending off her pushing.

"It was those *damn foreigner* girls, wasn't it? They're the ones who showed you!"

Father interjects, "Everything that happens to your son is your responsibility, Judy. Don't go around blaming others. It's called responsible parenting."

Mother stares daggers at him.

"Parenting?!" she screams. "Who's the one who encouraged him to play music? Who's the one who connected

Michael with that sleazy executive and that...that...*damn foreigner* band?"

"Stop saying that term, Judy!"

"This is what happens when you're around hippies," she yells at me.

I watch Mother whisk into my room and come out with my electric guitar.

"No, Mother!"

Though she's much smaller than me, Mother overpowers me from reclaiming it.

"Go into your room and write about how sorry you are in your diary," she commands. "Admit your mistakes and promise yourself that you'll never do drugs again!"

"C-can I have my guitar back?" I plead.

"No!"

I storm into my room, slamming the door so hard it bounces back open. I sit defiantly in front of my desk with a blank diary entry facing me. As my parents' screaming intensifies, I unfold my hands and jot down loose thoughts. Most of the words are incomprehensible, even the date is marked June thirty-first instead of July first, nineteen sixty-eight. I've never heard Mother and Father argue so fiercely.

Suddenly, a sound I wish were not true stabs my heart.

There's a large smash followed by the intertwining strings of my electric guitar. My blood boils so high, I unleash an inhuman yell. The loose words of my diary become 'KILL KILL KILL." I snap my pen in half, almost piercing the page. There's a large ink splatter next to the last 'L'. I rise and find my baseball bat, coming out of the room and pointing it at Mother.

"You dare?!" she screams. "I'm your Mother!"

Father immediately comes and takes the bat away.

"No. Come on!" Mother points. "Give that bat back to him! Let's see if this boy dares hit me! He's nothing but an *accident*! All that's happened today is an *accident*! The consequence of the biggest *accident* all those years ago!"

She steps on my broken guitar for effect. Father screams back at her and my mind feels distorted, not bearing the noise and staring at the broken guitar.

"I raised him on my own!"

"I did my best to help! I could've left! This was my house, Judy!"

"You're just like every *damn foreigner* — hiding his intentions with a mask of goodwill!"

I sweat profusely and stare at Mother who keeps screaming *damn foreigner* and *accident*. Every now and then she stomps on the corpse of my guitar and I look back with boiling rage.

"*Damn foreigner*! You and the *accident* ruined my life!"

At this, I lunge for the bat, trying to tear it away from Father's grip. I want to kill Mother. I'll show her the fury of an *accident*! I'll reveal the consequences of taking dreams away from this *accident*! Father flings me back and I drop to the ground, hitting my head to the wall. My hands are still removed from the bat. Everything's blurry. Mother repeatedly curses at Father.

"*Damn foreigner*! You and the *accident* can go to hell! *Damn foreigner*!"

As my vision adjusts, I see the hulking blot of my father marching up to the diminutive blot of Mother and, in disbelief, see the blot of my baseball bat rise and come down for an instant splatter. My breathe intensifies as I shake to comprehend what I've witnessed. The sudden silence answers my fears.

"Mother...!" the words escape me.

I hesitantly walk to the crime scene and spot a massive pool of blood that covers the back of her head. Father stands paralyzed, removed from reality. I see Mother's dripping blood from the bat's edge. As though I can miraculously save her, I remove my shirt and wrap her head, wanting Mother to come back to life.

Father slowly recovers and reaches for the phone, dialing 999.

My emotions pour and I hold Mother's body, crying. *Mother* is the only word I can say for the next hour.

When the ambulance arrives, Father and I are withheld as participants of a homicide. My expression's blank; my hands are continuously trembling.

"Michael," Father mutters. "It was me that broke the guitar."

I slowly turn to him, trembling at the realization that only he would have enough strength to break the guitar that way.

We're detained for the night at the police station. The strong typhoon winds sway and shake the walls. I'm released two days later, but Father remains in jail. The following afternoon, I join Mrs. Wilson and my step-sisters to see Father, but the police tells us he only wants me.

I'm taken to a small room with a table in it. Two guards watch us from a distance as I silently sit across Father. He looks older — lengthy beard, prominent strings of gray hair.

His thin, tired look suggests he hadn't eaten in the past days.

"Everything'll be okay," smiles Father. He holds my hands and adds, "I'm a former commander and British. They'll go easy on me. I won't be in jail for life."

"Father, I'm sorry I lost my temper that night. If I hadn't —"

"Stop it, Michael. Stop it. Look at me. What's done is done. If anything, I should be the one responsible for controlling my emotions. I'm responsible for this, you understand? Not you. Me." He sighs. "Besides, if it had been you that night, you'd be jailed for life. They'll go easy on me. Not you."

I nod, appreciating that Father could find something positive in this dire situation.

The case is a big financial hit to the Wilsons. They hire the best lawyer to see if Father can move his trial from Hong Kong. The jury won't go easy on him because he killed a local, despite his English stature. Since I'm a key witness, I fly to London to attend his trials, but Father remains jailed and it isn't until years of delays and re-trails that Father is finally free, though penniless. His pensions have all been suspended and his notorious record prevents him from finding decent work. Mrs. Wilson and my step-sisters have remained in Hong Kong without much contact to Father. Even I give up on him, pursuing other avenues of life while he waddles in severe alcoholism.

Eventually, I live permanently to London.

When I hear of his wintry death, I arrive nonchalantly before the ambulance arrive, looking at his pathetic corpse scrawled at the bottom of a stony stairwell.

He tripped, I'm told.

I find a coincidental similarity between his death pose, much resembling the likes of Mother — hair soaked in blood, lying face down to the ground. It's like nature took a baseball bat and pummeled him, head first into the concrete. The snow and blood contrast like a Rorschach. I look at its pattern, trying to make out what I see, but all I interpret is apathy.

The detachment remains at Father's funeral, but when I get home, the tears come out. I don't know exactly why, perhaps because I believe it's the fate for *accidents*. I don't pity Father, nor do I desire him. I'm sad that the dream of a real family was never possible from the beginning. I don't know why I cry — I just do.

I'm now college-aged without an education. Father's situation has placed me on welfare; he'd promise me that I wouldn't be in jail for life, but I constantly feel trapped. I look at the other recipients of welfare and I don't want to be like them.

Fortunately, Mrs. Wilson comes to my aid.

She mentions a lifelong promise and prides herself in honoring it. With her help, I finish a four-year degree in finance and find a decent job. There, I meet my current wife and with her family fortune, start our Chinese restaurant together. After my father-in-law passes away, we inherit his entire wealth.

Now we're caught up to the present.

The combined diary is finished.

A heavy burden is lifted, but I feel an unexpected inclination to be rid of this memento. As long as the words are written, I realize, the past lies beyond the heart's confines. It's not like I feel all the effort from the past few days are wasted, but I know my mission's incomplete.

I must dispose of all the diaries, including this new one.

The hotel restaurant manager is surprised to see me with the box of journals. I kindly ask his staff to incinerate them.

"Oh no, we can't do that, sir," the manager declines. "It could be a fire hazard and we're too busy at the moment anyway. However —" he takes out a lighter. "Why don't you go to the back near the barbecue pits and use that area to burn your books. The open area would be more suitable for that sort of thing."

I thank him and take his advice.

At the barbecue pits, I tear each diary page and set them on fire. I watch them crumble like tiny knots, each disappearing from my troubled past. The wind picks up the new ashes and scatters them to oblivion. I'm pleased. During one of the last diaries to burn — Father's – a little note slips from the side jacket. I must've missed it during my re-reads. I pick it up from curiosity, quickly dismissing the contents as mere routine topics, but the letter is signed "Wilson, James". The handwriting is different, extremely distinct from the previous scratching of Father's diaries. I open the one I'm holding and compare.

Indeed, they're different.

As I stand trying to figure out this newfound mystery, a staff member approaches me with a letter. It has to be from Susan or her husband — they're the only ones who know I'm here.

I quickly tear the envelope and read the letter.

Suddenly, I need to postpone my leave.

Come early next morning, I make my way to the one-story stone house and pause to admire the "Silver Forest Studio" sign.

"Come in, the door's unlock," musters a weak voice.

It takes me awhile to adjust to the dark interior, but I make out a very old man — the same old man who tried to give me the artwork many days ago — and he is calmly sitting on a beaten sofa. The room is silent with merely his labored breathing.

Then he breaks the ice.

"I'm sorry I wasn't here yesterday. I was at the hospital."

I nod in understanding.

"You know, Michael, I don't leave the door locked because it makes it easier for the paramedics. There's nothing to steal, I'm a simple man with simple solutions."

He stops and takes in deep breaths.

"My condolences to your declining health," I muster.

"Ah," he waves off. "Old men like me are always ill. It's the nature of life."

William makes an effort to get up. I rush over and help him.

"Thank you, Michael. You see, I've known you since the day you were born. If my math is correct, you're now sixty-three years old, correct?"

I chuckle admiring his sharp mind.

"Yes, sir."

William begins retelling the same story about Mother and Father. Out of politeness, I listen for awhile, then slowly steer him from the painful past.

"Mr. Chen," I eventually get to my visitation's purpose. "Can you tell me which one of these is my father's handwriting?"

I expose the letter and one of Father's diaries. William fumbles around for his reading glasses, then, putting them on, examines both items.

"This note is certainly your dad's handwriting. I'd recognize it anywhere."

"Remarkable" I compliment. "It's amazing how you're able to recognize it all these years."

It's funny how I've never seen Father's handwriting before; he was always at work or drunk in a bar.

"So..." I point at the diary. "Whose handwriting is this then?"

The diary is one of the earlier ones, the time when I was a child. William inspects a few pages then snaps it shut.

"There's nothing in here but slander," he shakes his head.

"What do you mean?"

"Your mother isn't like this. She's depicted as a husband-stealing fiend. And that handwriting — I can *definitely* recognize that anywhere."

I blink, still lost in his hint.

"That woman. She still dots her i's in that silly loop, cross her t's in that exaggerated stroke. Just like those letters she used to write me when your mother and I first moved to England. It says in this diary that your mother used her letters to extort that *damn foreigner* woman. What a shameful lie."

"Mrs. Wilson," I slowly understand.

The old man suddenly stands up and I help him, but he quickly dismisses my aid, compelled to walk to a corner of the home and grab something from the dark.

"Margaret," he explains walking back. "Was an emotional woman — arrogant, mean. But she was also a good person. She just let a lot of sentiment get to her."

He slowly places the rolled up drawing in my hand.

"This is for you, Michael."

I shake my head, "William, I must apologize, but I don't have any room for it in my luggage. It'll be crinkled."

"Just look at it then," he insists.

The portrait is unrolled and decades of dust pop at me. I cough and almost drop the drawing, but then, I glimpse the artwork and open my mouth shocked. It's the same couple I'd seen several times in my view gazing...the man with the easel and the woman with the cerulean dotted umbrella.

"But...this drawing must be very old," I question.

"Of course it is. I drew that when I was dating your mother. That's us in the picture."

"And that's the old police station...back before it got turned into the Tai O Heritage Hotel," I express. "There's the cannon too."

"Yes, Michael. I never finished it until very recently."

"Because it rained that day when you originally drew it."

Williams eyes widen.

"How'd you know that, Michael? Did your mother tell you? I never told a soul."

I feel it's better to tell a lie than attempting to rationalize the supernatural.

"Er, it's just a wild guess, Mr. Chen. A lot of artists stop drawing because of sudden rain. It's quite common."

The old man sighs.

"For the longest time, after knowing what happened, I found it too painful to finish it. Your mother and I were so pure back then. I finally found the courage because it came from love."

We stand admiring the drawing for awhile, then a question pops in my head.

"That day...when you approached us and tried to give me this — how did you know who we were?"

The room is suddenly filled with Mr. Chen's labored laughter.

"Michael," he chuckles. "Your step-sister is a dead ringer for her mother. You, on the other hand — with that hair and those eyes...and your flat nose — you're an obvious work of James and Judy."

I blush, embarrassed not to think of such an obvious

explanation.

We catch up on small talk then bid ourselves farewell. He insists on walking me to the door, puffing and wheezing.

"I'm so happy to talk with you once more in my lifetime," he shows a toothless grin.

"The pleasure's mine, Mr. Chen."

With William's artwork in hand, I nod and return to the hotel.

My plane finally arrives in England and I rub my soles on the ground to make sure I'm really here: the present. My wife, children and grandchildren greet me and I'm reminded of how foolish I am to feel lonely and family-less. *Accidents* have a purpose. It's foolish to hang onto regrets — without tragedy, certain happiness cannot exist. Life is filled with strange ironies.

All I can find is peace in its mess.

Inside a taxi, I grow sleepy as my wife fills me on things that happened. She takes the carefully rolled-up drawing from my hand and admires it.

"Hey, what's this? Did you get this from one of the galleries at Tsim Sha Tsui?"

I close my eyes.

"Why'd you waste money on such retro artwork? Look at the dress on this woman! It doesn't even go well with our wallpaper."

I tune her out.

"Hey, isn't this your mother when she was young? It looks like your description of her."

I focus on nothing.

"Er...it's pretty in its own way, I suppose."

I find that spot of perfect harmony.

"At least you'll finally have a portrait of your mother even if it's a drawing."

I absorb its embrace.

"Amazing how the artist was able to make it under such short time. Totally, custom job, I'm sure."

My soul's a clean slate.

"Hey, I'm talking to you. You awake?"

I'm free.

END